RAILROADS PAST AND PRESENT

George M. Smerk and H. Roger Grant, *editors*

DERAILED
by Bankruptcy

Life after
the Reading Railroad

Howard H. Lewis

Foreword by
John C. Spychalski

INDIANA UNIVERSITY PRESS
Bloomington & Indianapolis

This book is a publication of

INDIANA UNIVERSITY PRESS
Office of Scholarly Publishing
Herman B Wells Library 350
1320 East 10th Street
Bloomington, Indiana 47405 USA

iupress.indiana.edu

The paper used in this publication
meets the minimum requirements of
the American National Standard for
Information Sciences–Permanence of
Paper for Printed Library Materials,
ANSI Z39.48–1992.

*Manufactured in the
United States of America*

*Library of Congress
Cataloging-in-Publication Data*

Lewis, Howard H., [date]
    Derailed by bankruptcy : life after the
Reading Railroad / Howard H. Lewis.
    pages cm. — (Railroads
past and present)
    Includes bibliographical references
    ISBN 978-0-253-01866-3 (cl : alk. paper)
    — ISBN 978-0-253-01871-7 (eb) 1. Reading
Company. 2. Railroads—United States—
Finance. 3. Railroads—United States
—Management. 4. Bankruptcy—United
States. 5. Railroads and state—United
States. I. Title.
    HE2791.R27 L49 2016
    385.06'57481—dc23

                                    2015014883

1 2 3 4 5   20 19 18 17 16 15

To my family, my wife and children who bore with me while I did the work which is the subject of this book.

CONTENTS

FOREWORD

Financial failure enveloped most of the rail network in the northeastern United States and adjacent territory during the first half of the 1970s. By 1973, seven companies operating a total of 25,160 route miles of line in this area were conducting business under bankruptcy law protection. Historically, most railroads that suffered bankruptcy were returned to solvency by so-called income-based reorganizations that reduced the claims of security holders to levels that could be sustained by existing and estimated future levels of revenue. However, the situation in 1973 was different. By then it had become apparent that the existing and foreseeable earnings of most if not all of the seven bankrupt companies had fallen too low to support a reorganized structure of debt and equity securities of any magnitude. Consequently, liquidation of the companies' assets and termination of most of the rail service in the Northeast became a real threat, thus posing the specter of serious collateral negative economic consequences, locally, regionally, and nationally.

This grim scene sets the stage for attorney Howard H. Lewis's autobiographical portrayal of his involvement with the bankruptcy proceedings of the Reading Company.[1] As operator of 1,149 route miles of line comprising 4.5 percent of the aforementioned total of 25,160 miles, the Reading ranked third in size among its bankrupt counterparts. Although dwarfed by the 19,300-mile Penn Central Transportation Company, largest of the bankrupt carriers, the Reading served customers for whom continued availability of rail freight service was either absolutely essential or highly preferable vis-à-vis motor freight service. In addition, the Reading operated heavily used commuter passenger service in portions of the greater Philadelphia area, where diversion to private automobile usage was generally considered unacceptable from a net public benefit perspective. Perhaps more importantly from the perspective of rail industry competitive structure and rail freight service users, Reading formed a key link in connection with the Central of New Jersey (51 percent owned by Reading) and the Baltimore & Ohio portion of the Chessie system that countered the post-1967 dominance of Penn Central in the Northeast, particularly in the New York metropolitan area.

Three events beyond the Reading Company's entry into bankruptcy law protection (on December 28, 1971) were pivotal in setting the course of professional and personal events that dominated Mr. Lewis's life through the almost decade-long progression of the Reading Company's bankruptcy case. First was the engagement of Mr. Lewis's Philadelphia-based law firm, Obermayer, Rebmann, Maxwell and Hippel (ORM&H), as counsel for the Reading's bankruptcy proceedings. Second was Mr. Lewis's ascendance to partner in ORM&H in 1972. Third was an evaluation of the performance of ORM&H's work for the Reading from the time of its start that Mr. Lewis performed at the request of the firm's managing partner. When presented with the finding that the Reading needed more "hands-on legal representation," the managing partner immediately reassigned leadership of the firm's Reading engagement to Mr. Lewis. Mr. Lewis accepted the assignment, albeit after first protesting in vain that he "hated trains." He anticipated that he could fulfill it without a large commitment of time by forming a team of subordinates who, in consort with members of the Reading's in-house legal staff, would fully meet the company's legal service needs.

Subsequent realities ultimately proved otherwise. In 1974, during the early phase of his involvement with the Reading case, Mr. Lewis's other duties grew with his appointment as head of ORM&H's Corporate Department. That position carried the responsibility for assigning and supervising work on all of the firm's corporate law–related engagements. Simultaneously, his Reading-related work continued on an upward trajectory. Constraints on available resources forced him to take and maintain a direct hands-on leadership role throughout the duration of the Reading case. The demand on his time and energy that it imposed rose to a level that overshadowed his efforts on behalf of his other duties within ORM&H well before the closure of the Reading Company's bankruptcy case in 1981. His personal time was also virtually eliminated. Regular presence at family meals and other activities became impossible, communication with his children and spouse diminished, family vacations were foregone, and in one instance almost all of a Christmas Day (1980) was even consumed by his frantic effort to meet an urgent Reading case work deadline in lieu of participating in long-standing traditional family activities.

At the heart of the book are the author's revelations about the many conditions and problems he dealt with, the personalities he encountered, and the actions he took throughout his years of work on the case. The impossibility of bringing the Reading out of bankruptcy by means of an income-based reorganization obviously made it impossible for the company to continue to exist as a provider of rail transport service. This left only one objective for the company's bankruptcy trustees and their legal counsel to pursue: to obtain funds from the sale of the company's assets that in the aggregate would (hopefully) enable the settlement of creditors' claims and the distribution of any residue funds to shareholders. Howard Lewis's "inside story" of how this objective was ably achieved should be instructive and even entertaining for readers interested in corporate bankruptcy law, railroad financial and managerial history, and government transport policy.

John C. Spychalski
Professor Emeritus of Supply Chain Management
The Pennsylvania State University

ABBREVIATIONS

CERL   Combined Erie, Reading, and Lehigh
Valley Railroads (existed only in the
mind of the US government)

Chessie   Chesapeake and Ohio Railway and affiliated
companies, including the Baltimore and Ohio
Railroad and the Western Maryland Railway

CNJ   Central Railroad of New Jersey

CMV   constitutional minimum value

Conrail   Consolidated Rail Corporation

CUE   compensable unconstitutional erosion

Erie   Erie Lackawanna Railway

FRA   Federal Railroad Administration

ICC   Interstate Commerce Commission

IPO   initial public offering

NRO   net railway operating income

OCLDD	original cost less depreciation and deterioration
P&E	Peoria and Eastern Railway
PG&N	Philadelphia, Germantown and Norristown Railroad
Rail Act	Regional Rail Reorganization Act of 1973
RCNL	reproduction cost new less depreciation
Reading	Reading Railroad
SEPTA	Southeastern Pennsylvania Transportation Authority
USRA	United States Railway Association

IMPORTANT NAMES

Arthur Baylis   provided testimony as to the
     valuation of the Reading Railroad

Isabel Benham   valuation expert for the Reading Railroad

Charles Bertrand   president of the Reading Railroad

John Brennan   chief financial officer for the Reading Railroad

John Bunting   CEO of First Pennsylvania Bank

Joseph (Joe) L. Castle   trustee of the Reading Railroad
     (succeeding Richardson Dilworth upon Dilworth's death)

Lloyd Cutter   lawyer representing the Penn Central Railroad

Richardson (Dick) Dilworth   trustee of the Reading Railroad

William (Bill) Dimeling   attorney for the Reading Railroad

William (Bill) Ditter   judge in charge of the
     Reading Railroad's reorganization

Richard (Dick) Duzak   accountant with Peat Marwick

Herbert A. Fogel   mentor

Lockwood (Lock) L. Fogg Jr.   special counsel and later
    secretary and general counsel to the Reading Company

John Fowler   attorney for the Reading Company

Jim Frick   former Reading Railroad employee (returned
    to help tie up loose ends after conveyance)

Henry Friendly   chief judge of special court

William Fuchs   managing partner of Obermayer,
    Rebmann, Maxwell and Hippel

Jim Gallagher   accountant with Peat Marwick

Alfred (Bill) W. Hesse   senior vice president and general
    counsel, and later president, of the Reading Company

Tom Keyser   chief financial officer of the
    Reading Railroad after John Brennan

Andrew (Drew) L. Lewis   trustee of the Reading
    Railroad and later secretary of transportation

Bernard (Bernie) G. Meltzer   real estate broker and
    local columnist and radio personality

Christine Nethesheim   attorney for the United
    States Railway Association

Hugh Scott   US senator

Doug Segal   attorney for the United States Railway Association

Larry Shiekman   partner at Pepper, Hamilton
    & Scheetz, representing Conrail

James (Jim) Alan Sox   assistant to Howard Lewis and
    former law clerk of Judge William Ditter

Grant Sprecher   head of the Litigation Department at
    Obermayer, Rebmann, Maxwell and Hippel

Roszel Thomsen   judge of special court formed to
    oversee the railroad's reorganization

Stuart Warden   former Reading Railroad employee
    (returned to help tie up loose ends after conveyance)

Harris Weinstein   attorney representing
    Penn Central's passenger case

John Wisdom   judge of special court and
    Fifth Circuit Court of Appeals

DERAILED
by Bankruptcy

Introduction

I am, by nature and inclination, lazy. Like many, I came to the practice of law with no great vocation but rather for its place as a refuge for the humanistically educated and verbally inclined. I had small talent and even less training. I graduated from Harvard Law School without distinction and accepted an offer from the firm for which I had clerked. After six and a half years, it became apparent to me that I needed to move on.

I was then hired by the law firm of Obermayer, Rebmann, Maxwell and Hippel in December 1969 and became a partner in 1972. I was appointed head of the Corporate Department in 1974. Under the firm's culture, as department head I had the responsibility, or better the privilege, of assigning and supervising all corporate work as it developed, which meant I could keep the best and most lucrative work for myself while assigning the less rewarding cases to others. I had it made. Then there came the Reading.

For those of you who have forgotten your Monopoly, the Reading is, or was, a medium-sized bridge carrier centered around Reading, Pennsylvania, with lines extending south to Wilmington, Delaware, northwest to Newberry Junction (Williamsport), Pennsylvania, west to Harrisburg, Pennsylvania, northeast to Newark, New Jersey (in partnership with the Central Railroad of New Jersey), and east to Philadelphia and, in combination with Penn Central, Atlantic City.

The Reading Company had a glorious history.[1] It was once the largest corporation in the United States and focused on carrying anthracite, or hard coal, from the mines of Schuylkill County, whose county seat is located in Pottsville, Pennsylvania, to the port of Philadelphia for transshipment up and down the east coast and, to a lesser extent, Europe. It was a highly integrated vertical monopoly, building most of its own locomotives and some cars at its shop in Reading; it also owned much of the coal it shipped until it was forced to divest itself of the coal mines as a result of an antitrust decision in 1923, spinning them off to its shareholders in a company known as the Reading Anthracite Coal Company. It had a violent history of labor warfare, culminating in the prosecution and execution of the Molly Maguires at the hands of its then president, Franklin B. Gowen. Its financial history was no less stormy; it suffered through several bankruptcies in the late nineteenth and early twentieth centuries, which it solved in the traditional manner of railroad bankruptcies by giving its bondholders and other creditors stock for their debt. Finally, it figured prominently in the eastern railroad wars in the first half of the twentieth century between the Pennsylvania Railroad and the New York Central. If it could be said in the period before the New Deal that the Pennsylvania Railroad owned the Pennsylvania legislature and the Pennsylvania Supreme Court, at least the Reading owned Schuylkill County.

All of this past glory had long faded by the time I became involved in the Reading's affairs in 1972. At that time, 51 percent of its stock was owned by the Chessie, an amalgam of the Chesapeake and Ohio, Baltimore and Ohio, Western Maryland, and a few other minor roads. It served as Chessie's access to markets in Philadelphia through its main route from its connection with the Western Maryland at Lurgan (which is a cornfield), to Allentown, to connections with the Lehigh Valley and Delaware and Hudson, and through there to markets in New York and New England. It also went up the Delaware River to a connection with the Central Railroad of New Jersey (which Reading controlled through stock ownership) and then to the so-called Chemical Coast, that line of drug and chemical industries in northern and central New Jersey which produces some of the most lucrative as well as hazardous rail car loads in the country; out of all its lines, its single most profitable move was transshipping ore from the port of Philadelphia to Bethlehem Steel's plant at Bethlehem, Pennsylvania. It was essentially an arm of the Chessie

acquired cheaply through a controlling, but less than total, stock ownership, and served as an important chip in Chessie's struggle to compete
with what was then the giant Penn Central, a merger of the Pennsylvania
and New York Central roads.

This book is a memoir and not a history. To attempt a history would
require a great deal of research in sources outside my own notes, written presentations, and memory. This work is primarily a record of my
experience, not an analysis of the transformation of the rail industry,
and as such, it does not pretend to be a complete objective account of
what happened.

1

The Age of Innocence

My first experience with the Reading was learning in 1971 that we at ORM&H would be counsel for it in its recently filed reorganization, and wasn't that exciting? It didn't really excite me. From what I casually learned about the case, it seemed to be a litigation, not a corporate matter, and I expected to have little if anything to do with it.

In the winter of 1972–1973, my mentor, Herbert A. Fogel, who was in charge of the Reading account, decided to ascend to the federal bench, and shortly thereafter my managing partner, William Fuchs, asked me to look into the representation to make sure that our client was being serviced adequately. I dutifully reported that I sensed some unhappiness in my short meetings with Reading's staff and Drew Lewis, its active trustee, and that their affairs could stand some more hands-on legal representation. He turned to me and said, "OK, you're it."

"But Bill," I replied, "I hate trains."

"You'll learn to love them, Howard. Besides, you have enough independent means to be able to afford a large commitment of your time at low rates to something that will end one day with no follow-up."

"All right, I'll try, but only until I can find someone else."

At the time I thought I could go in and organize a team consisting of a corporate associate, a government liaison, and a litigator, all of whom would devote small amounts of their time to specific problems, while the Reading, under its own legal staff, would run itself and I could become essentially a figurehead. This was the first of many errors on my part, for I found that, like Br'er Rabbit and the Tar Baby, the more I touched it, the more it drew me in. Still, this was a gradual process. I remember going home after an early meeting and telling my wife that I had the Reading. She asked if I knew a lot about railroad law. "Nothing whatsoever," I told her. "They've got a legal department, and as trustees' counsel my job is sort of to look self-important, collect fees, and assign specific help for specific tasks."

Still, from those early months came the one decision of mine that really mattered to the eventual success of the enterprise. At that time, and earlier, there existed an attitude among those employed in large private law firms that the dregs of the profession ended up working for the government (federal, state, or local) or in corporate legal departments. This misconception has long since vanished, but it infected my two predecessors. Our first lawyer in charge of the account treated the Reading staff attorneys as virtual errand boys, fit only to get coffee, on the grounds, I suppose, that they were mere house counsel and, what is worse, that if they'd been any good at all, the railroad would not have gone bankrupt. His successor, the man who preceded me, employed a different tactic. He was the soul of courtesy and affability, but he had the habit of summoning the senior Reading lawyers to meetings in our offices at 8:00 AM, at which he wouldn't appear until 7:00 PM. He would call in during the day, saying that he was tied up with Senator Hugh Scott (our then counsel to the firm) or John Bunting (then CEO of First Pennsylvania Bank) or some other mythological figure. Finally he arrived, made a few largely irrelevant comments, rescheduled the meeting for some later date, and then departed, thereby wasting the entire day of two pressured, busy men. As one of them said to me later, on being called forth to meet they simply grabbed whatever they could from their desks so that they could so something with their days.

By contrast, I was not terribly interested in asserting my own self-importance. It seemed to me that if we were to have any chance of success at all, I had to forge with Reading's lawyers a relationship of complete trust and confidence. They knew the property; the two top attorneys had over seventy combined years of railroad law experience. I would have been idiotic not to have tried for the greatest possible cooperation, which, I thought, could only be founded on mutual respect and courtesy. What I did not expect, but for which I will be forever grateful, was that the respect and courtesy ripened over time into a kind of love, such as a son has for a father.

I wanted to instill the idea that I was there to learn, not to bully; that I knew nothing really about the Reading and was dependent upon them for all the understanding of the operation I would need. The first sign of change in this relationship was in how, when, and where we met. I always came to their offices—where, after all, the papers and other personnel that might be needed were located—instead of summoning them to mine. I always tried to arrive early. I let it be known that I was anxious to meet with them to discuss what they thought was important, rather than summoning them to deal with my agenda, which would have been rather foolish since at the beginning I didn't know enough to formulate an agenda. The result of this attitude was that I developed two friendships and as close a professional relationship as I have ever had. By the end of the eight-plus years in which we were in daily contact I could tell by the tone of their voices when Lock or Bill said yes in support of some fool idea of mine even though they really meant no, and we would discuss it. Most often they were right.

As I remember, from a distance of now more than thirty years, Alfred (Bill) W. Hesse, the Reading's senior vice president and general counsel, and later president, and Lockwood (Lock) W. Fogg Jr., senior counsel and later vice president for law, I am struck by, among other things, how different they were from me. Perhaps it was a generational thing (they were both thirty years older than I was), but for whatever reason, they had a very different view of the law. They were both driven by a sense of the law in the abstract, a love of its formality and precision as a thing apart from the purposes it served. By contrast, I am more result oriented, ready to use all ethical means to effect an end. Physically, they were both thin, wiry men, prominently bespectacled; Bill was more outgoing and humorous, which showed in his face, while Lock was more obsessed with accuracy, which gave his face a kind of mask that only really disappeared after two Manhattans, when his fundamental kindness and joviality came to the fore.

I felt that as the trustees' lawyer my contact with Reading's management should be through and with its lawyers. I saw no reason to get independently close to Reading's other management, from Charles Bertrand, its president, to the senior vice presidents, let alone others further down the line. Indeed, I saw myself as becoming more of a nuisance than a help had I done so. On the other hand, I felt I had to get to know the trustees, my clients.

I had never met my namesake, Andrew L. Lewis Jr., until my first trustee-management meeting. I knew him by reputation as a powerful force in Pennsylvania's Republican Party and as Senator Richard Schweiker's campaign manager. When I did meet him he seemed a small, unassuming man with a politeness stemming from innate good manners, while at the same time projecting a sense of quick understanding and organizational control. Annoyingly, though two years older than I was, he looked younger, and there were a number of people involved in the case, including some lawyers for the government, who assumed I got the representation because I was his older brother. It took me some time before I recognized how able and forceful he was.

At an early meeting, Drew turned to me and said, "Howard, my co-trustee Dick Dilworth isn't feeling very well these days, so he's been missing some meetings lately. I want to take you over to his office so you can meet him." Dick Dilworth was for me a very different figure than the then-unknown Drew Lewis. In the late 1940s when I was twelve or thirteen, Dick Dilworth was an awesome presence. Already a legendary trial lawyer as head of his own powerful firm, he often used to meet late into the night in my parents' house at 1916 Spruce Street with Joe Clark, Walter Phillips, and others to plot the demise of the Republican machine's control of the city of Philadelphia. Until my bedtime, I used to make drinks, collect glasses, clean out ashtrays, and listen with rapt attention to the words of the great man. Time passed; I went to boarding school, college, graduate school, the army, and law school, and began my practice. He became district attorney, a brilliant reforming mayor for two terms, unsuccessful candidate for governor of Pennsylvania, and a dominant leader in Philadelphia whose reputation and influence extended far beyond the city. Our paths seldom crossed.

As Drew and I were walking from the Reading Terminal at Twelfth and Market Streets to the Dilworth office at 123 South Broad Street, I turned to him and said, "You know, Drew, I sort of know Mr. Dilworth. I'm not sure it's necessary for me to formally meet him."

"No, no," Drew said. "Come on—I want him to know you're on the team."

As we walked into his office, Dilworth turned toward us, and with a politician's sure instinct he recognized me immediately and said, "Howard, what are you doing here?"

"Well actually, Dick, I'm your lawyer." Before taking me by the hand and saying graciously, "That's wonderful—I'm sure you'll make a great addition," I'm certain I saw in his eyes the memory of the pimply-faced twelve-year-old kid passing drinks. Within six months, he was dead. (I like to think it was a case of *post hoc,* not *propter hoc,* but I've never been quite sure.) Upon his death, he was succeeded as trustee by Joseph L. Castle, a well-respected local banker who had done work as a court-appointed master for Bill Ditter, the judge in charge of Reading's reorganization, who chose him.

Soon afterward, in the spring and summer of 1972, my work for the Reading began to fall into a fairly easy routine, and I began to know a little bit about the cast of characters. The early work consisted chiefly of getting rather routine administrative petitions approved by the court: payment of attorneys' bills (other than mine, which were then subject to Interstate Commerce Commission approval); permission to sell some small parcels of property and lease others; permission to buy equipment; permission to pay consultants; and a host of other matters associated with running a railroad, which under Section 77 of what was then the Bankruptcy Act had to be approved by the court. The Reading staff, usually Lock Fogg or someone under his supervision, would prepare a batch of such petitions on a biweekly basis. I would review them and present them in court with a brief summary of my own. The judge would ask if anyone wanted to be heard on the matter, and when invariably no one did, he would approve them. Hardly a terribly challenging procedure; the only goal was to get the whole thing done as expeditiously as possible. Nevertheless, I will not forget my first appearances in this exercise, as they were also my first appearances in federal court—or indeed any court—other than the chambers of a bankruptcy referee, the predecessor to the bankruptcy judge under the new code. Small things troubled me. I really didn't know where I was supposed to sit—at which counsel table, on which side of the bench. I arbitrarily and instinctively picked the table nearest the door and was never questioned about it.

In retrospect, this period prior to the end of 1973 seems like that period of stillness and quiet that often precedes a major storm. I basically reacted to problems Lock and Bill presented to me, read and wrote a few contracts, handled a few more-than-routine petitions. I was not terribly committed to the client, nor were the trustees. Dilworth was dying and Drew was busy campaigning for governor of Pennsylvania. The operation more or less ran itself, continually at a loss.

There was one matter which was not routine. The Reading had a substantial passenger operation comprising a commuter service from central Philadelphia to its northern and western suburbs, which was a disastrously money-losing venture, and a single intercity passenger service from Philadelphia to Newark, which was uniquely profitable among American passenger rail services at the time. The Philadelphia-to-Newark run largely served New York's garment district, picking up its passengers in the morning from the stations near their homes in Jenkintown and Elkins Park and delivering them home at night; the bar car was extremely active on the way back, and was perhaps in large part responsible for the route's profitability. This intercity line was of no real concern, but the commuter service, by contrast, was an enormous problem; in the opinion of many it was the fundamental cause of the railroad's bankruptcy. In an effort to find a solution, the railroad had negotiated a document called the "Memorandum of Understanding" between itself and the Southeastern Pennsylvania Transportation Authority (SEPTA), the basic intent of which was to transfer to SEPTA the service and the rail lines over which it ran, in exchange for relief from the obligation of providing the service, including maintenance of the applicable right-of-way, but no additional money. By the time I arrived on the scene, enthusiasm for this project had waned, at least on the part of the Reading. Although the agreement had promised relief from financial hemorrhaging, it had several problems, which in a way epitomized the basic difficulty of the entire reorganization.

The lines which provided the passenger service also had freight service over them. And so, if SEPTA were to own the lines, what share of the freight revenues from the lines would it be entitled to? The answer to this would have been complex, since some traffic originated on the lines, some terminated there, and most simply passed over them as a connecting link to other points of the system. Further, the Reading, like other railroads in the region, was not a single entity but leased a good deal of its trackage from other entities under 999-year leases. Typically these companies, after entering into such leases, became shells with no obligations but to collect the rent and distribute it to their shareholders. As investments, they were prized by trust officers as having a slightly better return than government bonds and being just as safe. The Reading had four such: the Delaware and Bound Brook Railroad Company; the North Pennsylvania Railroad Company; the East Pennsylvania Railroad; and the Philadelphia, Germantown and Norristown Railroad Company (PG&N). In railroad parlance, they were all termed "underliers," companies that owned rights-of-way but did not conduct operations. All of them shared an office and a single corporate secretary, and three of them at this time shared a single law firm, though each had separate presidents and directors who received modest fees for even more modest effort. Indeed, the presidencies and directorships of these entities were plums awarded by the banks to well-born scions of proper Philadelphia families whose trusts were administered by the selfsame banks. With bankruptcy, however, the rent vanished, and the bank-appointed officers were thrust into activity.

When the rent ceased, the trust officers panicked and bailed out of the stock of these companies for peanuts. The bankers and the old ladies they serviced were replaced with aggressive, hard-nosed speculators and arbitrageurs who acted very differently from their genteel predecessors. Trying to get them in line behind a coherent plan of action proved difficult. Our new trustee Joe Castle, since he was a banker, volunteered to handle the problem. As an opening move, he set up a lunch meeting with Drew, himself, and Pat Cestaro and his colleagues at Oppenheimer and Company who controlled the North Penn, the largest of the underliers, with Bill Hesse invited along to help smooth things over. After the meeting, I asked Bill what happened. "Well, Howard," he said, "it didn't go too well. After half an hour of contention, Joe exploded, turned to Drew, and told him they couldn't deal with idiots like these and that they were leaving. Drew protested that he hadn't finished his bagel. Joe insisted, grabbed his briefcase, threw open the door, and stormed out. Unfortunately, it was the wrong door and he stormed into the broom closet. Mrs. Davis, the secretary for all the roads, turned to him and said, 'Joe, as long as you're in there, why don't you clean the place up?' Then we all left, somewhat deflated and defeated."

Each of these companies, particularly PG&N and the North Penn, had extensive ownership over the passenger lines, and in the context of the Memorandum of Understanding were not about to give up their property (which technically reverted to them on the Reading's default under the leases) for no compensation. For these reasons, the memorandum was quickly left to die, though not without some grumbling on the part of SEPTA.

With the struggle over the Memorandum of Understanding, I began to get some feel for the cast of characters and for the ambivalent roles that the trustees and I as their counsel were destined to play. Our difficulty stemmed from the trustees' charge both to keep the railroad operating to provide service to the public, both passenger and freight, and at the same time preserve value for the creditors and the stockholders. By and large, the government parties, the federal government acting through both the Justice Department and the Interstate Commerce Commission (ICC), both Pennsylvania and New Jersey (Delaware, where the Reading line also extended, was inactive in the proceeding), all municipalities, the labor unions, and individual shippers favored continuation of the operation until a reorganization plan or governmental solution could be worked out. The creditors (except for the state and local taxing authorities who wanted their money but not at the expense of loss of service) generally favored shutting the railroad down and selling its assets, rail, railroad right-of-way, other land, shops, cars, locomotives, and a plethora of miscellaneous assets, including a trucking company and a telegraph company. The stockholders were a special case. The Reading was more than 50 percent owned by the Baltimore and Ohio affiliate of the Chessie, which wanted the operation to continue but was unwilling to assume any obligation or exposure in connection with it; the other stockholders were not organized and were unrepresented as a group, but were less than enthusiastic about the prospect of daily losses and daily deterioration of the value of their investment.

The argument between those who wanted the railroad to continue and those who wanted to scrap it antedated the filing of the petition of bankruptcy as the financial condition of the Reading and most railroads in the Northeast began to deteriorate. Though some railroad-owned real estate was very valuable, railroad right-of-way is essentially worthless except as a railroad, even ignoring the problem of title. Still, the railroad was losing money on an operating basis, generating negative NROI (net railway operating income), and the claims against it were mounting on a daily basis.

Bankruptcy, of course, heightened this dispute and provided a forum and procedure for addressing the argument. The first battle in this war was fought before I entered the field. Very shortly after filing the petition, Kelley Drye & Warren, the attorneys for Manufacturers Hanover Bank, the trustee under Reading's corporate indenture, representing the large insurance-company owners of the bonds (an impressive, well-suited band of New Yorkers) descended upon the trustees for the purpose of carefully explaining to them why it would be in the best interest of everyone if the Reading were shut down. Dick Dilworth, who embodied the image of a refined Philadelphia gentleman, listened to them for a while and then said in his upper-crust, well-modulated voice, "Ah yes, gentlemen. I see. You're going to ask the bankruptcy judge to discontinue operations, to eliminate rail service from a great many small and not-so-small businesses, to eliminate competitive rail service from such large operations as Bethlehem Steel and U.S. Steel at Fairless, to strand some 1,800 daily commuters in Philadelphia. Know what I think he's going to tell you gentlemen? I think he's going to tell you to go fuck yourselves." There was a stunned silence and the meeting broke up. Years later, one or more of the creditor representatives said to me, "You should have been at that first conference with Dilworth. After he told us to modify our sex lives, we didn't really know what to say."

They regrouped, however. The battle over whether to keep the rail-road operating was refought over and over again. Once again, it was joined formally before I got into the case. It was repeated every time we renewed the lease with SEPTA and every time we sought an extension of time to file a plan of reorganization. The issue was to some extent novel in that the bankruptcies of the 1960s and '70s differed from earlier rail-road bankruptcies. In the earlier bankruptcies, the problem was almost always excessive debt and debt service. The railroads made money on their operations, but not enough to pay the interest on their bonds and other long-term debt, or in some cases taxes. The solution was simple in design, though often highly complex in execution: convert the debt in whole or in part to equity and give the bondholders stock. By contrast, the bankrupt railroads in the early '70s were not profitable as operations. Absent interest payment on debt, absent payment of all taxes, given less maintenance of track and equipment than was necessary let alone desir-able, and given nonpayment of judgments for personal injuries, the rail-roads were still losing money. Heroic efforts were necessary to maintain a barely sustainable positive cash flow. Nevertheless, the trustees took the position that the operation must be maintained if possible. As Drew once said to me, "Our goal is to last one week longer than Penn Central." This position was not so one-sided as it might appear. It looked for a public solution, which the trustees and I felt necessary in order to avoid a catastrophic transportation and economic breakdown, and recognized that the proceeds of a liquidation for scrap were inherently much less than the potential value of a profitable rail operation. We were of course right, say I with the benefit of hindsight, but the issue was not clear then.

Being right, somehow, is not always the same as being believed. There were a number of creditors who simply looked at the amount of land the railroad controlled, without regard to the state of the title, took a look at Penn Central's properties at Park Avenue in New York, leapt to the assumption that our properties must necessarily be of the same kind, and reached the conclusion that if we would only quit running the trains we would become vastly rich from the sale of the land. There were several problems with this. First, the bulk of the property was railroad right-of-way, which is not really very valuable. As one Reading executive said in reply to creditor harassment, "You're absolutely right. Now all we need is a developer who wants to put up an apartment complex one hundred feet wide and eleven hundred miles long, stretching from the slums of Philadelphia through the boondocks of Pennsylvania." Second, most of our major properties other than right-of-way consisted of yards and other holdings in highly depressed areas of North Philadelphia. Nothing like the Pam Am Building or the Biltmore Hotel was in our inventory. Finally, Reading owned little of its property outright, as most of it was controlled under various easements or leases. The state of that title became increasingly important as the case developed and will be revisited in later chapters of this book. At this point, we all had a tendency to ignore it to the extent possible, seeing no benefit to us in an elaborate discussion of title analysis.

The focus of the battle over liquidation versus preservation was the periodic review of the SEPTA lease. In hearing after hearing, the judge permitted us to renew the lease, but we all felt the increased pressure he was under as he kept authorizing us to lose more and more money and let the creditors' position continue to worsen. We were all under pressure to find or at least attempt to find some long-term solution.

It was at that point that I began to appreciate the judge before whom I was appearing. William Ditter is a small man, not imposing on first sight, but as I came to know him over the years we worked together, my respect for him continued to grow. Not intellectually flashy, he almost always came to the right conclusion (which I admit was often the point of view I urged on him); never loud or domineering, he projected an aura of quiet, reasoned authority. I have always believed that it is wrong for a lawyer to try to get personally close to a judge before whom he is appearing in court, that such personal contact puts a judge under even greater pressure than that which is inherent in the office and function itself, and for that reason is unfair. That said, I came to love him, though at a distance. After the case was over we became even closer than we were while it was going on, and "Bill" Ditter, as I now referred to him, very kindly officiated at my second son's wedding.

The year 1973 opened dismally and closed on a note of hope, to some extent reduced by a measure of uncertainty. Throughout that year, we attempted a variety of solutions which largely went nowhere. We revisited the Memorandum of Understanding between Reading and SEPTA, designed to relieve Reading's enormous losses stemming from its commuter passenger service, but the only relief SEPTA felt it could offer was far too little to do much good. Also, under the aegis of the hearings that Congress began to conduct on the rail problem in the region, we attempted to formulate a merger among ourselves, the Central Railroad of New Jersey (CNJ), and Lehigh Valley under the theory that eliminating duplicative service and redundant lines might result in enough cash savings to make the combined road, which was christened the Mid-Atlantic Railroad Corporation (MARC), marginally profitable. Though this attracted mild interest from our partners, particularly Lehigh Valley, and though we made some preliminary studies, in the end nothing came of it. What did occur, however, was the outline of a federal solution created by the Regional Rail Reorganization Act of 1973, effective January 1, 1974. The act looked toward the creation of a federally owned and controlled railroad called Consolidated Rail Corporation (Conrail), comprising all the bankrupt railroads in the region.

While all this was brewing, Drew took me aside once again and asked, "Howard, do you know how you got this representation?"

"No, Drew, not exactly."

"Well, it was like this," he said. "When Bill Ditter asked me to serve as trustee, we both chose Dilworth on the theory that the whole thing would wind up as a political matter and we needed a well-connected Democrat. At the same time, I wanted to be governor of Pennsylvania and the endorsement of your counsel Hugh Scott was essential. As I said to Dilworth, 'You can pick the accountant and everyone else, but I need to pick the lawyer,' and that's how you got the Reading. Now I've run for governor and lost. In the meantime, you've had some good fees and my debt is paid. I'll keep you on but if you make even one mistake, you're out. I'm sure you're a good lawyer and I'm sure your firm is a good one, but there are lots of good lawyers and lots of good firms, and some of them can do a lot more for me than you can."

I liked him immediately. I dislike bullshit, except of course my own.

The Rail Act created a complex scheme to affect the transfer of rail assets from the bankrupts to the new federal railroad. I will elaborate on a number of the provisions in the appropriate places as this narrative unfolds, but what struck me initially was the provision establishing a "Special Court" to oversee the transfer of assets and the fairness of the compensation to be given to the transferors for those assets. This meant that the whole process would be an enormous consolidated litigation involving all the bankrupt railroads on one side and the government on the other, before a special selected panel of judges. As I reflected on the Special Court process, my feet got colder and colder. I went to the head of our Litigation Department, Grant Sprecher, and said, "Look Grant, the Reading has just become a huge lawsuit. It will involve preparation of testimony, marshaling of evidence, cross-examination, and a whole lot of stuff I know nothing about. You're the litigator, not me; I'm a corporate lawyer. It's time you took over."

He replied, "Look, Howard, you tell me the evidence will involve discounted cash flows, risk analysis, labor protection estimates, and a whole lot of stuff I know nothing about. Besides, you tell me that the case will probably be tried on a paper record by way of depositions and trial examinations outside of court. You'll be able to get away with tactics I wouldn't dare try."

"What you're really telling me is that you have no intention of endangering your lucrative medical malpractice defense practice by devoting five or more years to walking down a dead-end street."

He grinned sheepishly. "I'll help."

That help amounted to a total of about five hours of hand-holding and advice over the course of the litigation, plus his taking responsibility for a number of tangential matters, such as our suit to get value for our Trailer Train stock. Still, the hand-holding was invaluable, making me feel somewhat less alone and less desperate.

Among the other annoyances of the Reading representation was that it was extraordinarily low-paying. Under former Section 77 of the Bankruptcy Act, the Interstate Commerce Commission was given authority to approve the bankrupt trustees' counsel fees. By a chain of arcane reasoning which discounted or eliminated the private law firm's need to cover overhead—a matter to which, as government lawyers, they were totally oblivious—the ICC stressed the partially pro bono nature of the work, made some other assumptions about efficiency, and thus came up with an hourly rate slightly less than what I was paying my plumber.

Since my own compensation was directly tied to the amount of money I brought in, I felt this deeply.

Miraculously, there appeared a sign of hope.

In late 1974, Congress passed a bill making certain relatively technical amendments to the Rail Act. Buried among the generally ambiguous and incomprehensible verbiage typical of amendating acts was a stroke of genius widely attributed to Harry Sileck, counsel to the Erie, which relieved the ICC of the intolerable burden of reviewing and approving our fees. With a whoop of joy shared by all other counsel to the railroads in reorganization, I scheduled an appointment with Drew as senior trustee to increase our rates to something less than, but close to, normal charges. He met me in his office wearing, for the first and last time, as far as I know, his Gerald Ford WIN button ("Whip Inflation Now"). He took my hand in both of his, stared at me with his china blue eyes, and said that the rates fixed by the ICC were an outrage, an insult to hardworking professionals; however, his position in the Republican Party demanded adherence not only to the letter but also to the spirit of the presidential guidelines. I said I understood his position perfectly, thanked him for listening to me, picked up the requisite number of tickets to the next Republican fundraiser, and left. I managed to withhold the tears until I was out the door.

2

The Gathering Storm

After the passage of the Rail Act in January of 1973, I decided it might be a good idea to read it. The act introduced an entirely new concept into American bankruptcy law: the idea of dual reorganization. Under it, the rail operations of the several railroads in bankruptcy in the region, defined as the northeast quadrant of the United States—namely, the Penn Central (much larger than the rest of the roads combined), the Reading, the Lehigh Valley, and the Central Railroad of New Jersey (all roughly the same size), the Ann Arbor and the Lehigh and Hudson River (much smaller), and later the Erie Lackawanna (smaller than Penn Central but much larger than Reading)—were to be split off from the remaining properties of the bankrupts and formed into a new government-controlled railroad called Conrail. The remaining properties were to continue in reorganization under Section 77, from which the creditors and possibly the stockholders would receive relief in the form of stock, cash, or new debt in many possible forms. The bankrupts would also be given interests in the new railroad in compensation and substitution for their transferred rail properties.

So peculiar was the concept of dual reorganization that a great many people never understood it. At one point in an opinion affecting the Reading, a judge of the Third Circuit stated that "the railroad was no longer being reorganized under Section 77 but under the Rail Act." I wondered at the time how he thought the opinion he was reviewing from the Section 77 Reorganization Court had come into being. I remember too being told by opposing counsel in an ancillary matter that no one ever heard of a dual reorganization, that it couldn't exist. Yet the concept seems to me to be not that difficult. There is no reason, for example, why a portion of a large shopping center in bankruptcy cannot be condemned by a local government for a school; the bankrupt stands in the same position as any other condemnee so long as it gets fair compensation for the property taken. Admittedly, there is the jurisdictional problem of who is to determine the value of the property taken—the court supervising the condemnation proceeding or the court supervising the bankruptcy. The Rail Act met this problem by placing responsibility for the evaluation of the property conveyed in a Special Court created by Section 209(6) of the act. In addition, the Special Court was also charged with valuing the batch of Conrail securities given in exchange for that property. For example, if the court determined, after weighing the evidence, that a rail property had a value of one hundred million dollars, then it also had to determine if the Conrail securities offered in accordance with the act also had a value of one hundred million dollars.

The first valuation was of an existing entity valued either for scrap consisting of ties, rails, and land for sale for nonrail purposes, or as a going concern valuable to another acquiring railroad as a railroad. The second valuation was akin to valuing a start-up, that is, the question of what would be the new entity's (Conrail's) ability to generate profit.

Before getting to the problem of dual valuation, someone had to determine what properties of the bankrupts should be taken to form the new railroad. Obviously, if all the properties of all the bankrupt railroads were taken, the same duplications and inefficiencies that were a major cause of the failures of the individual roads would be incorporated into the new railroad. To solve the problem, Section 201 of the act created a new federal agency called the United States Railway Association (USRA), whose primary responsibility was to create a "Final System Plan" (Section 206). In addition to some high-sounding platitudes about environmental integrity, preserving rail transportation for the communities affected, etc., the essence of this section provided that the association would determine which properties would be conveyed to the new railroad, Conrail, under Title 3 of the act, in exchange solely for "stock or other securities of the Corporation [Conrail] including obligations of the Association [USRA]."

The next problem confronting the drafters of the act was how to handle the separate reorganization proceedings of the seven bankrupt roads so as to prevent collateral attacks on the scheme in the several reorganization courts. To that end, Section 207(b) of the act provided that within 120 days of the act's effective date (January 1, 1974), "each United States District Court or other Court having jurisdiction over a railroad in reorganization shall decide whether the railroad is reorganizable on an income basis within a reasonable time under Section 77 of the Bankruptcy Act (11 U.S.C. 205) and *that the public interest would be better served by continuing the present reorganization proceedings than by a reorganization under this Act*" (emphasis added).

Thereafter, within 180 days after the effective date of the act and 60 days after a report from the Rail Service Planning Office set up by Section 205, "each United States District Court or other Court having jurisdiction of a railroad in reorganization shall decide whether or not such railroad shall be reorganized by means of transferring some of the rail property to the Corporation pursuant to the provision of this Act." There followed language about the importance of the public interest and essentially the direction that each reorganization court should approve reorganization under the Rail Act unless it "finds that the Act does not provide a process which would be fair and equitable to the estate of the railroad in reorganization in which case it shall dismiss the reorganization proceeding [under the Act]" but not the Section 77 reorganization, which would continue. Both decisions required something of a crystal ball, since they were to occur before USRA was required to produce a Preliminary System Plan (300 days after January 2, 1974—Section 207[a]) or the Final System Plan (420 days after January 1, 1974). The reorganization courts were thus asked to approve unknown transfers of rail property to a corporation not yet formed, for unknown amounts of stock in that corporation at a time when it was impossible to value that stock. Some of us had some trouble with that.

The third essential ingredient of Title 2 of the act was the creation of the Special Court charged with the dual valuation described previously.

The genius, or perhaps better, evil genius, of the act was exemplified in this provision for the Special Court. It characterized the act not as a condemnation statute where the bankrupt estates' compensation fairly clearly would have been in cash, but rather as a reorganization statute whereby the estates would become owners together of an entity, which consisted of a combination of parts of all of them, simplified and improved. In short, they would still be in the railroad business but without any ability to control their own destiny, and, above all, with no government cash awarded them. Appeals from the Special Court were directed to the United States Supreme Court.

The creation of the Special Court rested on a preexisting foundation which had been fashioned after special-purpose courts in the past. Thus, "within 30 days after the date of enactment of the Act, the Association shall make application to the judicial panel on multidistrict litigation authorized by Section 1407 of Title 28 United States Code, for the consolidation in a single three-judge District Court of the United States of all judicial proceedings with respect to the Final System Plan" (Section 209[b]). The staffing of the Special Court in some ways was a more important undertaking than its creation. Some eight or nine years later, after all the sound and fury was over, at a symposium held by the Historical Society of Pennsylvania on "original intent in interpreting the Constitution," Judge John Wisdom told me what happened:

> I was in charge of the multidistrict panel when the Rail Act was passed, so the job of finding the people was mine. In common with everyone else, I wanted Henry Friendly as presiding judge due to his experience as a young lawyer with the railroad bankruptcies of the 1930s and his outstanding reputation as a judge in complex business and constitutional litigation. He agreed, provided he could have his old law school roommate, Roszel Thomsen, a federal district judge in Maryland, as one of the other judges. Thomsen was delighted. Then I persuaded Carl McGowan of the Court of Appeals for the District of Columbia to take the third place. Well, when McGowan realized that his entire life would be absorbed in railroading for the next five years or more, he fled. Then Henry called me up and said, "Look, John, you got me into this; you've got to be our third judge." So I was hoist by my own petard.

However it happened, I believe everyone connected with the case thought that there could not have been a better panel. Everyone was impressed with the ability of the court and with the judges' ability to work together.

As mentioned above, the first actions required by the Rail Act were the 120- and 180-day determinations by the reorganization courts as to whether or not some of the property of the bankrupts should be reorganized under the Rail Act and whether the act provided a process which was fair and equitable to the estates. There were a great many reasons for answering both questions in the negative. The rail properties were to be made available to USRA for inclusion in Conrail before the association determined which of the properties it wanted, what value it put on them and how the stock given in payment for the properties was to be valued pro forma, and finally whether or not Conrail could ever achieve a level of profitability to sustain those values. The reorganization courts were asked to foreclose all other options to dispose of the properties for rail or nonrail use, such as sales to profitable railroads or sales for scrap and land development. It seemed to many that for the trustees to take this gamble would be the height of folly and the abrogation of their duty to achieve the best value possible for the railroads' creditors. It also seemed to many that the Rail Act was a blatant attempt to use Congress's reorganization powers to subvert the "due compensation" clause in the Fifth Amendment to the Constitution—that, in short, Congress was disguising a condemnation or taking as a reorganization so as to avoid paying for the properties taken in cash, whatever the Final System Plan determined those properties might be. All of the trustees other than Reading's and Ann Arbor's urged their reorganization courts to decide the two questions in the negative, against the position of the government, which several of the reorganization courts did.

While recognizing the grave weaknesses and dangers in the plan promulgated by the Rail Act, I thought it might be better to work with what the government had given us than run the risk of the government's refusal to act at all. The Reading was losing money every day on operations, and the experiences of Penn Central, the Lehigh Valley, and CNJ were worse. Unlike previous railroad bankruptcies where the roads had positive NROI and their failures stemmed from their inability to pay interest on amortized debt, the bankruptcies of the 1970s were operating failures as well as financial ones. It had taken the government over two years to come up with this plan even though by the time it started serious planning it was clear that if nothing were done a total collapse of rail freight service in the Northeast was inevitable, which in turn would have caused an enormous national economic disaster. Further, as long as the government was in the field either actively pursuing the plan or passively considering other options, no other solution such as piecemeal sales to the profitable railroads like the Chessie or the Norfolk Southern was possible; no one would act until the government's position was clearly known. Therefore, it seemed to me that to reject the government's solution was to take an unacceptable risk of catastrophe. I called up Bill Hesse and outlined my thinking to him. "Thank God, Howard," he said. "I was terribly afraid you'd take a strict lawyer's view of the question and forget the mess we're in. We've got to go along. Further, if we say yes when the others say no, it might make it easier later for us to work with the government." I then filed the appropriate papers and memoranda urging acceptance of the government's plan. Judge Ditter signed the approval orders.

The next step, obviously, was the appeal of the several orders of the reorganization courts to the Special Court under Section 207(b) of the Rail Act. The appeals were duly filed and the case came on for argument on August 27 and 28, 1974. This was the first and last major rail case effort in which Judge Carl McGowan participated before being replaced by Judge Wisdom. The case was heard in the ceremonial courtroom in Washington, DC, before a huge audience, most of whom were charging time to one client or another, sometimes several. Indeed, the accumulation of lawyers' fees on those two days might well have in and of itself thrown a moderate-sized company into bankruptcy. Penn Central led the bulk of the argument against the constitutionality of the act, while naturally the government led the supporting parties.

At this point, I should identify the government legal team more precisely than "the government." It consisted of, first, a wholly newly created team of lawyers who were a part of USRA. In addition, there were lawyers from the Justice Department and the Department of Transportation. Finally, USRA hired three large and well-respected Washington law firms: Wilmer Cutler and Pickering, Hogan and Hartson, and later Steptoe and Johnson. One result was that a total of 175 lawyers for the government signed one or more court pleadings. As the case went on, I kept thinking of the Merrill Lynch and the "thundering herd."

The Penn Central parties' argument in a nutshell was that the compelled reorganization, which was the hybrid essence of the Rail Act, "failed as a bankruptcy proceeding because of the absence of judicial determination of fairness prior to the required exchange and as an eminent domain statute because of the lack of assurance of full payment." The basic problem was that the properties were to be conveyed for Conrail securities when there was no way to know whether Conrail's operation would be profitable enough to make the securities given to the transferring railroad "sufficient to constitute the constitutional minimum" value as required by the eminent domain provisions of the Constitution, or indeed any value. The court, gasping and struggling, found a way out by holding that in the event of a shortfall of value to the transferors, they could sue in the government in the Court of Claims under the Tucker Act.

I took a more simple position, pointing out that the Reading had done all it could reasonably be expected to do to effect an income-based reorganization under Section 77 and failed, and that though it was far from insolvent, it could not reorganize without help such as that provided by the Rail Act. Further, as long as the Rail Act existed or there was any other promise of federal help, private parties, including the profitable railroads, would be reluctant to step in and provide a private solution. In opposition, Manufacturers Hanover Bank, trustee for the senior debt, argued that the Reading was in such bad shape that the reorganization under Section 77 should be terminated and the properties liquidated. By contrast, the Commonwealth of Pennsylvania argued that the Reading was in such good shape that if ably run and advised, it should be able to effect a Section 77 reorganization. The court agreed with us:

> After giving full consideration (1) to the argument of MHT Co. that Reading is in such hopeless shape despite the relief offered by the Regional Railroad Reorganization Act that its reorganization should be dismissed, and (2) to the argument of the Commonwealth that Reading is in such good shape that despite potential competition with a revitalized P.C. [Penn Central], it can be reorganized on an income basis within a reasonable period of time under Section 77, we agree with the conclusion reached by Judge Ditter

(i.e., reorganization of the railroad under the act).

Though I rather anticipated the court's conclusion, which left the Rail Act intact and in partial control of our reorganization, the procedure, particularly the oral argument, gave me an opportunity to assess the entire picture and have some inkling of what to expect for the next six years. Frankly, the prospect was not a happy one. First, the courtroom was packed. Those of us who were the principal lawyers for the lead estates in the proceeding were few in number compared to the mass crowded into that large space. The vast majority of them were lawyers for railroads leased or operated by the lead carriers; lawyers for creditors' committees of the several estates; lawyers for the railroad labor unions; lawyers for public bodies such as the Commonwealth of Pennsylvania; a number of shippers with their lawyers; lawyers for profitable railroads likely to be affected by the process; and finally a large number of speculators and arbitrageurs hoping to glean from a word dropped here, a glance exchanged there, a hint as to which of the myriad equity and debt securities issued by the estates or their components and creditors might be undervalued, providing an opportunity for an alert vulture capitalist.

Second, I got a chance to inspect the judges, albeit at a distance. Carl McGowan gave every impression of a man looking for a seat in a crowded theater. Roszel Thomsen appeared to be thoroughly enjoying himself in the center of the overwhelming national crisis, wanting to be kind and respectful to everybody, to emanate goodwill but not about to take charge or provide the profound analysis necessary to formulate a solution to the novel and complex legal problem confronting the court. Henry Friendly, by contrast, appeared to be in complete control, to have already devised a solution. A relatively small man, then in his seventies, or so I guessed, he had a round cherubic face surrounded by a bush of unruly gray-blond hair. More noticeable, under heavy glasses, were a pair of blue eyes which were usually twinkling and benign but were capable of turning in an instant into an eagle's glare. He radiated an aura of cheerful politeness, generally going out of his way to compliment all of us to the delight of our own malpractice carriers. As I grew to know him over the years, I detected what I thought was a kind of world-weary bitterness, but above all, I and others got the distinct impression that we would be trying our cases to a single judge.

The oral arguments themselves, in which I did not participate, basically rambled on, covering the points outlined above, with Lloyd Cutter for the government arguing that any solution other than the Rail Act might be so expensive as to preclude federal participation even if that meant the collapse of the rail system. This was a totally hyperbolic statement. It did, however, give Judge Friendly the chance to point out that those who hoped that "billions [would] be awarded as a result of these proceedings [were] sadly mistaken." On that note, the arguments concluded, and as we all filed out I heard the man next to me say, "Well, this was interesting but of course irrelevant. The issues in this mess will be resolved by the Supreme Court on the appeal of the Connecticut General–Penn Central case that held the act unconstitutional. They'll come up with their own solution." I thought otherwise. Indeed, the Supreme Court in reversing *Connecticut General* in an opinion dated December 18, 1974, adopted both the reasoning and conclusion of the Special Court's October opinion. That was the last word the Supreme Court uttered on the matter. Somewhat later in the proceeding, two or three years I think, as various parties tried to take issues to the Supreme Court by petition for certiorari or direct appeal and found their petitions denied and appeals quashed per curium, the garrulous Justice Harry Blackmun told one of our members at a cocktail party, "If any of you lot think we're going to touch Henry on this one, you're crazy."

3

A Time of Waiting

Following the 1974 opinion came a time of waiting and regrouping during which nothing much happened of a formal nature until the government produced the Final System Plan as required by the Rail Act. During that period, however, we set about preparing for the oncoming deluge. One obvious question was who was going to try the case in the almost certain event that the government's offer of compensation proved to be inadequate. I remember receiving a telephone call from Paul Duke, then head of Penn Central's in-house legal department, asking what firm was going to try the Reading's case and who would be the lead litigator. I replied, "Well, Paul, I guess we are and I am."

There was a stunned silence. "Howard, I always thought of you more as a business lawyer. Have you had much litigation experience?"

"None whatever."

"I see. Well, we're going with the very distinguished firm of Covington and Burling in Washington with their superb Litigation Department."

"That's nice," I said. I don't think I made his day as he contemplated a gross amateur stumbling around messing up his case to the advantage of the government.

The basic work of the reorganization continued: the filing and approval of the routine petitions for payment of bills, vacating or affirming leases, and other ordinary matters attendant on the continuing, though losing, operation of the railroad. But it was during this hiatus that an event of great significance to the subsequent development of the litigation occurred. I received a long letter from Judge Ditter extolling the merits of one James Alan Sox, his former law clerk, who had been responsible for the Reading matters when he worked for the judge. Ditter praised Jim's analytical ability, his hard work, his writing skills, and his integrity, and said all the usual things one says about somebody one is recommending to someone else for a job.

Of course, I immediately called up Jim and invited him for an interview. I should have known who he was before he showed up—after all, he had been working on Reading's matters for some two years—but somehow he had not really made any impression on me. When he walked into my office I saw a small dark-haired young man who was understandably nervous. As we talked, I found him clearly articulate and sincere rather than glib. He described his experiences as an editor of the Rutgers Law Review and his work for the court with a gentle honesty, neither overly assertive and boastful nor overly self-deprecating, unlike most autobiographers. I liked him, though he was not really what I was expecting. After about ten minutes' conversation, I took him around to meet some of my partners, particularly Grant Sprecher, since Jim would be joining us primarily in a litigation capacity. After Jim left, I went back to Grant's office and said, "What do you think?"

"Look, Howard," he said, "I know we've got to hire him given that letter, but as soon as the Reading's over, he's out of here." Grant had sensed, as did I—correctly, as it turned out—that Jim was gay, and he worried that this would hinder Jim's ability to work effectively as a litigator.

"Look, Grant," I said, "I know we're under pressure to give him a job, but I'm not going to hire him on the basis you suggest. We're not New York. We don't take kids for special purposes and throw them out when the project is over, or they get too expensive or too close to the client. I'd like to hire him but on the same basis we hire every other associate, with the same opportunities and the same training and nurturing we give everyone else." I also thought Grant was wrong to be so concerned about Jim's sexual orientation—his intelligence and sincerity were impressive, and that's what would count with clients and juries. In the end Grant relented, said I could hire Jim, and agreed to give him the same shot at partnership as everyone else.

Jim joined us in the spring of 1975, and I found no problem at all integrating him into the Reading work. Both Bill and Lock seemed to work easily with him, though almost all of the client interface remained mine. As for the trustees, the only reaction I got was Drew's, "I hear you hired Ditter's law clerk. Smooth move."

For both Jim and me, our relationship was a new, rather strange one. For him it was his first real job; for me, it was the first time I had another professional working virtually exclusively for me. Previously, I had assigned various discrete projects to a number of people whom I supervised, some more closely than others. Most of the time I received a more or less finished product: agreements, wills, and briefs which I absorbed into my own work or legal memoranda. None of this involved a close personal relationship. I realized that what Jim and I were embarking upon would be different. We would have to work side by side on strategy, tactics, witness preparation, briefs, and whatever else the Special Court devised as it structured the case it was about to hear. I realized too that the work might well be harder in its demands for intellectual imagination and plain physical labor than anything either of us had ever done before. I made one resolution going in: whatever happened, I would work myself harder and spend longer hours than I would ever ask him to do.

In the lull awaiting the Final System Plan, there were other ancillary Reading matters to occupy us both before the reorganization court and elsewhere. One of the most bizarre was Reading's acquisition by way of lease of 1,200 hopper cars. Several years previously, Reading had obtained the court's permission to acquire these cars on the grounds that they were necessary to service our largest single shipper, the Bethlehem Steel plant at Bethlehem, Pennsylvania. We thought, or more particularly our then president Charlie Bertrand thought, that we could make a lot of money on them either in the Bethlehem service or leased out to other roads on a per diem basis.

As is characteristic of these deals, there were endless meetings in the offices of the New York lawyers who represented the financial entity created to exploit the investment tax credit available at that time. My only task was to make sure that the documents did not cause any liability to Reading when the cars were inevitably transferred to Conrail. The documents grew clause by clause, sentence by sentence, rather like fungi growing in the back of damp, dark caves. Semicolons were changed, commas adjusted. Nothing was ever deleted; everything grew and was padded out, including, of course, lawyers' time sheets. There were many of us—lawyers for Reading's bondholders, lawyers for the custodian bank, lawyers for the financial vehicle—all of whom had suggestions, changes, and endless revisions, as well as Lock Fogg, who (as a Reading lawyer in charge of corporate indenture) had been through this drill before in Reading's several bond issues. For me, it was a deadening, albeit enlightening, experience as the trust indenture and other documents were transformed from the difficult and obscure into the totally incomprehensible, where each self-contained article grew and lost connection with all other articles. All that was clear and certain was the passage of time and the mounting expense. Finally, we took delivery of the cars toward the end of 1976. Our president assured us that we did in fact make money on them, but by then the conveyance to Conrail had taken place and he was gone to take a job in Albany with the Delaware and Hudson.

4

The Beginning

Finally, in July of 1975, the government issued its Final System Plan, with a supplement issued in September. The plan followed a Preliminary System Plan dated February 20, 1975, which consisted of almost a thousand pages setting out in great detail the reconfiguration of the railroad system in the Northeast. In an effort to offer a sort of gesture toward maintaining competition in the industry, the Preliminary System Plan proposed a purchase by the Chessie of the Reading and the Erie. After considerable study on the part of the Chessie by a substantial team headed by one of its senior executives, James White, the Chessie declined the offer. That Chessie study became the foundation of our valuation claim in the case as it finally evolved.

The Chessie's rejection meant that the government's reorganization was to lead to Conrail, which would include all property "used or useful in rail transportation." It also invited an analysis of what precise property was in fact "used or useful"—what cars, locomotives, lines of railroad, yards, offices, etc.—a prospect that delighted the mass of lawyers assembled to represent either the government or the railroads in reorganization, now referred to collectively as the "transferors." The fights that ensued ranged from the fundamental to the silly. A few examples may illustrate the problem.

By way of preface, I will not deal with the enormous ancillary properties which everyone conceded remained with the estates. For the Penn Central, these included not only their clearly separate nonrail businesses such as theme parks, but also hotel and office buildings adjacent to Grand Central Terminal, the so-called Park Avenue properties. For us, in addition to a small trucking company there was the Reading Terminal and an adjacent office building plus the Reading Terminal Market, the whole constituting a rather derelict operation located in an area east of Philadelphia's City Hall which the city's modern revitalization had, quite understandably, passed by. I remember on several occasions during the course of the trial wishing to emphasize Reading's comparative poverty—referring to them ironically as "our Park Avenue properties." No, the conflict centered on assets more or less closely involved in the rail operations.

The properties to be conveyed to Conrail were detailed on large-scale section maps but in a very general fashion; what precise lines, yards, and other property actually necessary for the rail operation which had to be part of the conveyance, as opposed to peripheral properties that were to be retained by the estates and could be sold for real estate development (ranging from office space to a hot dog stand), remained to be determined. Under USRA's procedure, headed by a real estate lawyer named Doug Segal, Reading was allotted two days during which the precise metes and bounds of the conveyed lines were to be determined. A small team set forth from the Reading Terminal, consisting of our trustee Joe Castle, myself, and, I believe, Lock Fogg, bound for USRA's offices in Washington. We met in a small conference room with Doug, who elected to don a black robe in honor of the occasion. There were, in opposition to Lock and myself, lawyers for USRA, who wanted to make sure Conrail got enough land to carry out its freight operations, and Al Derr, who appeared for SEPTA to make sure that above and beyond the freight requirements there was enough land for possible additional passenger use. We wanted to keep as much land as possible; Conrail wanted to take as little as possible to minimize any payment to the estate; and Derr, who had no money on the table, was in an expansionist mode.

As we grouped around the table, Joe Castle may have had his finest hour. Just as we sat down, Joe turned toward us and said, "Look, I've had some experience in mechanical drawing as an undergraduate at Princeton—I'll take charge of the magic marker." Then, as "Judge"

Segal listened to what amounted to a great number of approximately four-minute arguments parcel by parcel and made his determinations, Joe would memorialize the decision on the section maps. If the actual line drawn in each instance tended to favor the Reading's position, well, so be it. For ten hours a day over two days, briefly interrupted for lunches eaten in the hearing room and provided by USRA, including beer courtesy of Judge Segal, the actual physical conveyance of Reading's property and the property of its leased lines to Conrail were determined. During the entire proceeding of conveyance, valuation, and litigation over the seven years it dragged on, this two-day event was hands-down the fairest, most cost-effective, and most efficient. We returned home exhausted but basically satisfied, and I never heard any complaint on the part of Conrail or SEPTA.

By way of comic relief and to give you a glimpse of the absurdity that occasionally found its way into the proceedings, I offer the following digression. In mid-December of 1975, to most people's surprise, the Special Court asked for statements of position on a procedural point so obscure, and to me so unimportant, that I immediately determined to ignore it. That decision did not last long. The same day I got the court's notice, Bill Hesse was on the phone: "Howard, when are you going to file your brief?"

"What brief? This issue is so far out I don't even know which side we should be on. All I do know is that whichever way it goes, it won't have any effect at all on the outcome of this case."

"I don't care. We're a small estate and we're going to be hopelessly lost in the shuffle while the court concentrates on Penn Central unless we make ourselves known and heard early and often. You're going to file a brief and appear at that hearing."

"Yes sir, and by the way, Bill, thanks, thanks a lot. I thought clients were supposed to control lawyers and minimize their time, not maximize it."

After a lot of reflection, I finally determined that there might be some slight advantage for Reading if the court ruled one way as opposed to the alternative. I therefore dutifully wrote and filed a brief and got Amtrak tickets to Washington for the appropriate day. I decided to go

alone since I couldn't really justify the expense of involving Jim in this
nonsense. When I arrived in the room located in the Court of Customs
and Patent Appeals, my analysis was confirmed. The only other party
to appear was the New Haven Railroad, represented by Joe Auerbach of
Sullivan and Worcester, which was a huge creditor of Penn Central as
a result of the New Haven's merger into that road and its failure to sell
its Penn Central stock when things looked good. The time set for the
hearing at 11:30 should have alerted me to its true purpose: the president
judge, Henry Friendly, wanted an opportunity at government expense to
have lunch with his old friend and law school roommate Roszel Thomsen, get to know Judge McGowan, and perhaps do a little tax-free holiday
shopping in the District.

He opened court with a broad smile, welcoming both Joe and me,
and said he'd read our briefs and was ready to hear our arguments, which
"should not detain us long." Joe got up and began: "Your Honor, this very
serious and complex case is essentially a Penn Central matter, which
you cannot possibly understand without at least a basic historical background. Now, in the early nineteenth century . . . ," and on he went.
Finally, after about forty-five minutes of increasingly irritated interruptions, Judge Friendly was at last able to gavel him down. The judge then
turned to me with what can only be described as a countenance inflamed
with ire and perhaps a missed lunch. "Now I suppose we have to hear
from the gentleman from the Reading," he said, likely assuming that I
would want to take at least as long as Joe.

I have seldom in my life wanted more to be someplace other than
where I was at that moment. I stood on wobbly knees, but as it does very
rarely, inspiration struck me: "Your Honor, my name is Howard Lewis.
I represent the Reading Railroad. It is but a small railroad, but there are
those of us who love it."[1]

The judge roared with laughter while his colleagues grinned benignly. "Are you a Dartmouth man?"

"No, Your Honor," I said with my best sycophantic grin. "Like you,
I'm Harvard, Harvard College and Law School." I then made my argument in less than three minutes and sat down to a glare from Joe Auerbach, one of the ugliest I have ever been given. In due course, we received
a ruling which, as I foresaw, had no effect whatsoever on the case.

My sense that I had done what my client wanted and incidentally made a favorable impression on the court did not last long. In the first serious round of briefing which took place about six months later, I got a call from the clerk of the Special Court, Richard Erickson, who told me that Judge Friendly was having a very difficult time reading my brief. My heart sank to the pit of my stomach; that's the last thing any lawyer wants to hear. I sort of stammered, "I'm sorry, Richard, I know I may not be the best writer in the world, but I thought my brief was marginally comprehensible."

"Oh no, no, Howard. It's not that he can't understand it. He can't see it."

"What?"

"That's right. It's not clear enough for him to make it out."

There began the only serious fight I ever had with Jim Sox. "Jim," I told him, "if I'm going to spend all the sweat and aggravation in writing this stuff, the least you can do is to produce it and send it out in visible shape. You're the Law Review kid, not me."

Jim fought back: "Howard, if this firm wasn't so cheap that it got all its equipment thirdhand at bankruptcy sales, maybe we could do something halfway professional around here. Besides, you went to Harvard; I'm Rutgers-Camden. That is good production as far as I'm concerned."

"Look, I don't care. I don't give a damn what you do. Have somebody engross the thing on parchment. Just send out a black-letter copy and make sure it never happens again."

In due course, after a clear copy was forwarded to the judge, I got a letter back:

Dear Mr. Lewis:
Thank you very much for the extra copy of your brief. It was indeed much clearer. It beats me how any lawyer could be so dumb as to spend a lot of time and effort writing a brief and allow his office to produce it in a form so unattractive for a Judge to read.
Sincerely,
Henry J. Friendly.

I took a long look at that letter, turned it over, turned it upside down, shook it, and decided I had really better share it with somebody. So I took it up to Grant and asked him to read it.

"Not good."

"No, not good."

"Do you think I should give it to the client?"

"No. Nothing substantive here at all."

"How about the malpractice carrier?"

"No. He's got enough on his plate already."

"Do you think I should put it in the main Reading file or file it sort of separately?"

"Oh. Separately, very separately."

There were other distractions during this prolonged period of waiting. Each senior member of Reading's organization had a pet idiocy I was supposed to promote and get through the reorganization court prior to conveyance to Conrail. First in line was Joe Castle. The Reading headquarters and principal station in Philadelphia occupied the better part of the north side of the block of Market Street between Twelfth and Eleventh Streets. In front of the station on the sidewalk stood a twelve-foot-tall metal tower holding a quadruple-dialed clock, facing in all four directions. The clock tower was, I suppose, relatively handsome and dated from the latter years of the nineteenth century; Joe loved it. He called me in one day and said, "Howard, I've been looking at what railroad memorabilia brings these days. That clock must be worth a fortune and we should get the judge's permission to sell it."

"Joe, let me see if I understand you," I said. "I'm supposed to get the clock specially excluded from the millions of specific items of all seven railroads to be conveyed to Conrail, and then what happens? Am I to get a permit to dig up the sidewalk, contract with a mover to haul it off to Sotheby's or Christie's for auction, or am I supposed to ask the judge to convene court on the sidewalk and auction the thing then and there, as is where is?"

"We'll work out the details later—the main thing is to get the clock."

"Another thing: how am I going to convince Larry Shiekman, representing Conrail, that the thing isn't used or useful in rail transportation? All stations have clocks—they're part of the mystique of rail travel."

"Don't be silly. Most people have watches, and besides, anyone who wants to can stand in the middle of Market Street and glance over his shoulder to see the City Hall clock."

"Yeah, that makes a lot of sense, particularly in rush-hour traffic."

Luck was on my side. Some three days after our conversation, the glass cover on the clock face pointing toward Twelfth Street dropped off and, as it shattered, slightly injured a number of passersby. Once Joe realized that the clock auction might be impeded by a number of small but vigorously prosecuted lawsuits, his enthusiasm for the clock sale waned and I heard no more about it.

My sense of relief was short-lived. A week or two after the clock fiasco, Drew Lewis called me on the phone and in his usual direct, no-nonsense manner said, "I want the table."

"Excuse me, what's this?"

"The boardroom table. I want it. I want it in my office at Plymouth Meeting where we're going to move the operation after conveyance."

"But Drew, office furniture is essential to the operation. Conrail may need the table."

"Look, they've got the Pennsylvania table; they've got the Central table; they've got the Erie table; they've got the Lehigh Valley table; they've got the CNJ table—for all I know, even the Ann Arbor and the Lehigh and Hudson River had tables. They don't need the Reading table. I want it."

My next trip down to the terminal, I looked at the thing. It was mahogany, large, ornate, overcarved, a kind of symbol of the time when railroad robber barons ruled the universe. As far as I was concerned, it was primarily a pain in the neck. Still, I dutifully called Larry, reminded him that I had gone out of my way to be cooperative with Conrail in this process, and begged. We got the table, but that was not the end of the matter. Bill Hesse reminded me that since Drew was taking the table for his private office, even though some Reading work would be done there the whole matter had the appearance of self-dealing and conflict of interest. Bill pointed out that we were very much in the public eye and in order to be squeaky clean, Drew had to pay for the table himself and should get at least three appraisals of value and accept the highest. "OK, Bill, whatever," I said. "All I know is I got Conrail to release the table—why don't you handle it from here?" The last thing I wanted to do at this juncture was infuriate my trustee-client. In due course, Drew got his table without any further involvement on my part.

Then there was Bill Hesse's pet project. This final and most difficult of these detours was both the most complicated and the most inconvenient of the lot, and it lasted well into the prosecution of the valuation case when none of us had time for anything else, let alone this distraction.

At some point in the antediluvian past, Reading had lent one of its locomotives, the Black Diamond, a classic example of the finest production of its shops circa 1920, to a transportation museum in St. Louis, Missouri. At a meeting ostensibly for the purpose of planning litigation strategy in our presentation to the Special Court, Bill turned to me and said, "Howard, the Black Diamond—we've got to get it back."

"What are you talking about?"

"The Black Diamond, our great locomotive. We lent it to a museum in St. Louis because there wasn't a suitable museum in Pennsylvania. Now there is, at Strasburg [the Railroad Museum of Pennsylvania]. Now they may think in St. Louis that the loan was supposed to be permanent, but it wasn't—the documents are unclear but I know it wasn't permanent."

"But Bill, don't we have more important things to do than fight with a museum over a lousy locomotive?"

"Howard, you don't understand. The Black Diamond symbolizes the Reading. It's beautiful and it's worth money which Strasburg as a state museum can pay to us in reduction of the taxes we owe Pennsylvania. You've got to go to court and get it back."

Dutifully, but reluctantly, I wrote to St. Louis demanding the return of the Black Diamond, threatening to cite them for contempt if they didn't give it back immediately. In due course, I got a phone call from a lawyer in St. Louis who was chairman of the museum's board. "Look," he said, "we can't give it back—we've built our main building around it. Besides, there's no way you can get it from St. Louis to Philadelphia or wherever in Pennsylvania you want it—the transportation will cost you many times more than it's worth."

"We've thought of that. We'll get a special FRA license and drive it up."

This had the desired effect of convincing the guy he was dealing with an absolute nut. "OK," he said. "Give me a week or so and I'll be back to you." Indeed, in a week I got another call and heard a rather desperate voice: "Look, I've scraped the bottom of the barrel out here, and the most I can come up with is fifteen thousand dollars. Will you take it?"

"Sold." I went to Hesse and told him I'd sold the Black Diamond for fifteen thousand.

"What? You can't do that. It's worth a great deal more. It has symbolic value—even as scrap it's worth more."

"Bill, we're trying to get two hundred million for Reading's rail property on a very tight court-imposed timetable. I can't work any harder and there's no money to obtain additional help and no time to familiarize them with the case even if the firm could spare them. Now you want me to spend days, weeks, arguing in court with a guy from St. Louis over what happened in the 1920s when we gave, lent, sold, or whatever that piece of junk to that museum?"

"Please, it is not a piece of junk—it's beautiful. But OK, OK, I see your point—you can get the court's permission to sell our heritage for fifteen thousand." It took virtually no time to work out a short agreement of sale drawn by the lawyer in St. Louis and get the court's permission and complete the transaction. Still, I fantasized about the image of me and Lock Fogg stripped to the waist shoveling coal into the Black Diamond's firebox while Bill, acting as engineer, got us lost in the woods of Ohio trying to reach Strasburg in the heat of August.

In the midst of the comic opera generated by my colleagues, that spring and summer there was one serious issue. Normal railroad operation entails not only the consumption of fuel, payment of crews' wages, and the like, but also the acquiring and scrapping of equipment. However, the Rail Act specifically conveyed not only designated land and track, but also supplies and equipment, such as freight cars and locomotives. USRA felt with some justification that as long as the railroads sold, scrapped, or otherwise disposed of equipment, it had no real fix on what it or Conrail would get at the date of conveyance. On the other hand, we felt that discontinuing our normal process of acquisition and disposition would be not only costly to us but also detrimental to Conrail, in that it would stick them with useless equipment and deprive them of material they needed.

Unfortunately, we were lead mule on this one. The Reading, in the normal course of its business, determined to scrap some four hundred hopper cars which had outlived their usefulness and had been more than replaced by the 1,200 cars in the transaction described in the previous chapter. When we filed in our reorganization court for permission to abandon the cars and conduct an auction to sell them for scrap, USRA, which received all copies of our pleadings, decided to bypass the reorganization court and moved in the Special Court for an order restraining us from proceeding. The decision to bypass the reorganization court in favor of the Special Court was, I suppose, tactically based on the notion, not altogether unjustified, that the trustees got from their own court pretty much what they wanted, whereas the Special Court was, among other things, charged with facilitating the conveyance process and would do pretty much what USRA wanted. Also, by moving in the Special Court, USRA sought to obtain a ruling that would apply to all seven railroads—not just the Reading.

Since the Special Court lacked a courtroom of its own, it held its hearings in a variety of borrowed rooms, generally in the Court of Customs and Patent Appeals in Washington, but this time in the federal courthouse in Philadelphia. Counsel for USRA and the other government parties argued with some insistence that it was the court's obligation to maintain the status quo so that USRA could know with certainty what the railroad they acquired would consist of on April 2, 1976—what tracks, employees, cash, fixtures, and locomotives and cars it would then have. I argued that the railroad was a living organism, that "status quo" meant in fact continued operations, which included payment of wages, purchases of supplies, collection of tariffs, payment and collection of interline charges, and, indeed, scrapping of equipment. At the end, I played my trump card and asked if any USRA representative had actually looked at the cars and determined if they wanted them and wanted to pay for them as part of the taking. The government was dumbfounded and had no response. Evidently, it never occurred to anyone to inspect the actual property instead of relying on the equipment lists maintained routinely by all the railroads. The court thought my request reasonable and withheld decision until the government had a chance to inspect the cars.

Some weeks passed and I heard nothing, so I asked Bill Hesse what had happened. "Oh, the government withdrew their motion," he said. "It seems when the USRA guy went out to the yard to look at the hoppers, one of the cars collapsed before his eyes in a pile of rust. I guess we hadn't used it in a while, say seven or eight years. At any rate, USRA decided they wanted no part of them." So ended that saga.

The next step was preparation for conveyance day. Though the Final System Plan was extensive in what it designated for conveyance, obviously it couldn't go into absolute detail for a variety of reasons. For instance, certain things could not have been known when the plan was written and only became clear when conveyance was imminent, such as the exact amount of accrued vacation pay assumed by Conrail or left as a charge upon the estate, the pension obligations of current employees, and the interline and per diem car-hire charges owed to and from other railroads. The list was long and the time for finalizing all these details was very short. We worked hard, fast, and in some cases intuitively, assuming that adjustments could be made later but that they should be as few and as small as possible.

Finally, John Brennan, Reading's chief financial officer, and I arrived at Judge Ditter's chambers a little after 5:00 PM on April 1, 1976, armed with a draft conveyance order, to meet with Larry Shiekman of Pepper, Hamilton and Scheetz, lawyers for Conrail. Though most matters had been negotiated earlier, there were still a couple of open items. We resolved our differences with great help from the judge in a fairly amicable manner, and the judge signed the order at about 11:00. John turned to me and said, "Howard, I feel great about this—we got pretty much what we wanted. Let's have some drinks."

"John, I'm sorry, I don't have any money. I've been in my office or here since seven this morning. I didn't get to the bank."

"Don't worry about a thing—before I came over here I ripped off petty cash. We've got lots of money."

I told that story later to Larry, who said, "You know, I'm not surprised. There wasn't a dime in any of those cash boxes. I wondered how they managed to buy coffee those last few days."

5

The Plot Thickens

With conveyance now past, everything changed. No longer charged with the obligations of providing rail service, both freight and passenger, the company became an entirely different entity. Instead of some two thousand employees, there were three people—Bill Hesse as president, Lock Fogg as secretary and general counsel, and John Brennan as chief financial officer—plus a very small support staff. In addition, there were the two trustees, Drew Lewis and Joe Castle, who were part-time, and me as outside lawyer with my staff, by which I mean Jim. Instead of occupying a large Edwardian pseudo-Moorish building at Twelfth and Market Streets in Philadelphia, the company had a small suite of offices at Plymouth Meeting, Pennsylvania. Instead of operating a railroad, the company devoted its entire energies to getting value for its remaining assets, above all its claim for compensation for the taking of its rail property into Conrail.

The assets, other than its claim, were principally a small, profitable trucking company, which it sold, some miscellaneous pieces of real estate, and the Reading Terminal Market and adjoining property, whose fate had to await the removal of the commuter service from the terminal. This was to follow the completion of a commuter tunnel linking the Reading and Penn Central passenger service, now, postconveyance, the sole responsibility of SEPTA. Still, unlike the Penn Central, these nonrail assets of Reading were of minor importance, so our claim against the government dominated everything else.

As time went on, Reading's staff increased slightly: John Fowler and Bill Dimeling joined to help with the reorganization procedures and the miscellaneous assets. Jim Frick and Stuart Warden, former Reading employees, came back to help tie up the myriad loose ends left after conveyance, such as payroll transfers to Conrail, pension administration, preexisting labor disputes, and the like. Still, the focus was on the claim.

As we contemplated our strategy for the case, the horizon looked bleak. Since we had negative NROI, a traditional reorganization where the bonded debt is converted to stock couldn't work because even then the Reading was a money loser. In that context, the government might well take the position that it had done us a favor by relieving us of our railroad operating obligation, and that therefore they owed us nothing. As it turned out, the government position was not far from that.

The government admitted that under the authority of a Supreme Court case, *Brooks-Scanlon v. Railroad Commission of Louisiana* (251 U.S. 9 [1920]), we could not be forced to engage in a hopelessly losing enterprise forever, but conceding our ability to quit the railroad business, they contended that our only alternative was to scrap the road and sell the property for nonrail uses, which position underlay their compensation analysis in the Final System Plan. They then assumed that since all the railroads subject to the Rail Act were in basically the same economic circumstances, we would all be scrapping our property simultaneously. This meant that the market would have a glut of such things as surplus rail to be sold for scrap steel, or wooden ties, whose only nonrail use was in the landscape gardening business. Even the value of real estate (though sold in specific local markets rather than general markets, as scrap steel or ties were) would be affected by these mass sales. The question we had was how best to oppose their arguments.

There were certain challenges we could mount to the government scenario of nonrail use or scrap. We could argue that all the railroads would not close down at the same time, so that the first railroad or railroads out could avoid the glut problem, but this had the obvious tactical disadvantage of pitting each of us against the others in a hard-to-envision hypothetical world. Everyone would want to be first. We could argue that the nonpassenger tunnels, which the government posited would have to be sealed off at our expense, could be sold to mushroom growers, who had a thriving business in southeastern Pennsylvania. None of these counterarguments, even if successful, produced much value.

The real estate, our largest asset, as was the case for most of the other roads, had its own problems. Aside from the office buildings and general open space constituting yards in urban areas, which had obvious value, most of the real estate was railroad right-of-way, which had value really only to the adjacent landholders. I kept remembering the exasperated executive's remark as to the desirability of a 1,200-mile housing development. In addition, we didn't actually own most of the right-of-way, a problem I dealt with later. In one respect, our job and everyone else's, including most particularly the Special Court's, had become easier. Once Conrail started operating, its losses exceeded those of all seven of the former roads put together, and so USRA was unable to assign *any* value to Conrail's stock. Thus, the Rail Act was further amended to provide "certificates of value" payable in cash for any shortfall between the value of the assets conveyed or determined by the court and the value of Conrail stock, which in essence eliminated the need to value Conrail.

The problems associated with the government's nonrail use method of valuation strongly suggested that we find some other hypothetical resale that would have occurred absent the Rail Act. OK, but what? It was clear that the industry in the Northeast was not viable in its then-existing form. All of the roads had the same negative NROI that Reading had, and the government, as hinted above, did indeed suggest that in relieving us of the obligation, it had in fact done us a favor. Also, *Brooks-Scanlon* left open questions as to when was "indefinitely" and what was "hopelessly losing," but at least it provided a framework for us to argue that at some point we were entitled to get some value some way for our properties. It occurred to me and Reading's management that if we could somehow ditch the passenger obligation, particularly the commuter trains from Philadelphia to its suburbs, and certain marginal lines only kept in operation because of the ICC's intransigence in refusing to let us get rid of them, and if we had an opportunity to renegotiate the labor contracts, there was a core of extremely profitable lines. These comprised lines serving traffic originating and terminating on the Reading and bridge lines that connected the Reading with other railroads. An example of the former was the line from Port Richmond in Philadelphia's northern waterfront to Bethlehem, Pennsylvania, where iron ore and coal were shipped from the dock over our lines to Bethlehem Steel's major mill. An example of the latter was the line from Lurgan, where Reading connected with the Chessie system, to Bound Brook in New Jersey, where it connected with the Central Railroad in New Jersey. This then gave Chessie access to the so-called Chemical Coast, where chemicals and pharmaceuticals from such companies as Monsanto and Hoffmann-La Roche were transshipped across the country. In short, we believed that there was a viable center that could have been made valuable and attractive to another railroad, particularly given opportunity costs.

Opportunity costs in general are both the enhanced value to an existing railroad such as the Chessie from the additional acquired lines and the loss of traffic over the railroad's existing property if a competitor should acquire those lines. Railroad rates are generally based on the number of miles that goods are transported. If an item of cargo is carried by an acquired line for ten miles and then by the acquiring road for an additional ninety miles, the gain in freight over the total is one hundred miles. Similarly, if the same cargo carried the same ten miles is diverted from its previous interchange to another carrier, the loss in freight to the former carrier is the ninety miles it used to earn and no longer does. USRA shared our belief that there was indeed a value in the Reading, which led it to offer parts of the Reading, combined with portions of the Erie, to the Chessie. The association made this offer not for the purpose of benefiting our argument, but rather because they were directed by the Rail Act to maintain rail competition in the region to the extent possible. In any event, the Chessie study became the basis of much of the evidence in our case.

There was another, larger problem to be surmounted before attempting a detailed, highly technical analysis of traffic patterns, costs, labor adjustments, and an infinite number of variables in order to demonstrate the value of the core. Why should the court or anyone else bother? The underlying argument that the government had done the bankrupts an enormous favor by relieving them of their public utility obligation to provide service, and that at most they were entitled only to scrap value for the property, simply would not go away. My objective was not so much to overwhelm the judges with a mass of incredibly complex and barely comprehensible evidence, but first to evoke sympathy for my client, to demonstrate that it was neither incompetent nor irresponsible but the victim of forces beyond its control, consisting of actions taken by the government itself. In short, the government screwed us.

I felt justified in my approach for a number of reasons. Perhaps most important in this case was the fact that the "evidence" presented would not be a careful analysis of what did happen, but a complex speculation on what would have happened if something (the Rail Act) that did happen had not happened. This meant, of course, that there was little or no reality check on the hypothetical worlds that we and the government sought to create. This left the government free to argue for the complete simultaneous scrapping of the entire rail system in the Northeast and us free to hypothesize a vast number of profitable railroads panting to purchase our core lines but having their desire frustrated by the Rail Act. There were moments in the course of the trial when I was grateful for my training in medieval theology. The lack of factual restraint meant to me that the court's sympathy was all-important, since it would have a huge range of theories and hypothetical facts on which it could rationally base any decision.

Fortunately, the court solved the problem of how best to present the sympathy argument by requesting pretrial briefings on the theories of valuation. It became clear in pretrial conferences and by the request itself that the court wished to block at the outset extreme theories of valuation. In doing so, it mentioned that it was confronted with a choice between two lines of cases. The first was an opinion by Justice Oliver Wendell Holmes Jr. (who also wrote the *Brooks-Scanlon* decision), *Boston Chamber of Commerce v. City of Boston* (217 U.S. 189 [1910]), which held that where there is condemnation for a public purpose the proper measure of valuation was what the condemnee had lost (in our case arguably nothing), not what the condemnor had gained (in our case arguably the preservation of the economy of the United States from collapse). In opposition to this line of cases was the opinion of Judge Kenneth Barnard Keating in New York in the PATH cases (20 N.Y. 2nd 437, 285 N.Y.S. 2nd 24, 231 N.E. 734 [1967] *cert. den.* 390 W.S. 1002 [1968]), which held that where a private enterprise has created a service which has become unprofitable but remains indispensable to a community, the measure of value of the property is, at least to some extent, based on its value to the community. If Judge Keating's rationale were accepted, one means of calculating value would be to calculate what it would cost the public that cannot do without the service to reconstruct it new, less the depreciation of the property, its wear and tear that had occurred over time; this theory was represented by the acronym RCNLD (reproduction cost new less depreciation). RCNLD, which included the cost of land acquisition (for example, in Penn Central's case, midtown Park Avenue in New York), yielded some pretty staggering numbers, way up in the hundreds of billions of dollars. Between these two extremes—nothing and hundreds of billions—the court pretty early on indicated a strong preference for nothing. My job, as I saw it, was to reverse that mindset.

Though industry failure is more often the product of multiple causes, I saw some justification in assigning a lot of the railroads' collective trouble to the government. Obviously, such reasoning appeared to be, and in fact was, largely self-serving. Still, there was enough objective evidence on which to evoke subjective sympathy for the industry. The three principal sources of government blame as I saw them were the subsidization of other forms of transportation; the intransigence and inflexibility of the Interstate Commerce Commission in approving changes, primarily mergers and combinations and abandonments of unprofitable routes; and unwarranted interference with labor relations.

To take these three causes in the order of their easiness to understand, the first is the subsidization of other means of transportation. The vast interstate highway system, begun in the Eisenhower administration and brought to near completion under Lyndon Johnson, while an obvious boon to the economy, presented a severe challenge to the railroads in that it made transport by truck much more efficient and attractive than it had been before the system was in place—first for the obvious reason that the system itself enabled trucks to carry goods throughout the country much faster and hence more cheaply than had been previously possible, and second because the user charges levied on trucks did not even begin to compensate the government for the cost of creating the system or even for the additional maintenance cost occasioned by truck use. In addition to what amounted to a trucker subsidy was the vast improvement to the country's airports, undertaken at local, state, and federal expense, which allowed the servicing of ever more efficient planes with gate slots priced to attract service rather than to recover construction costs. This made air freight transportation a much more competitive challenge to the railroads. Finally, the St. Lawrence Seaway, built and maintained at federal expense, diverted to ships a great deal of grain and ore traffic, long a railroad standby. All of this presented an enormous challenge to the railroad industry. But there was more.

Continually faced with the prospect of paralyzing nationwide railroad strikes, the government resorted to mandatory mediation, which distorted the negotiation process. Over time, managed agreements led to a bloated and overpaid workforce. When Reading entered bankruptcy, the standard freight train crew numbered five: an engineer, a fireman (terribly useful on a diesel locomotive), a conductor, and two trainmen. The last car on the train was a cute, boxy little thing called a caboose which allegedly served as a place of necessary rest for the crew, but which in reality was a traveling beer party and pinochle game. (OK, OK, so I'm not objective. This is a memoir.) By way of contrast and to skip ahead in my story, by the time Conrail was sold to the public, the standard crew numbered two—an engineer and a conductor—and the caboose had disappeared. In addition, the work rules instituted in the mid-nineteenth century remained in effect, so there were mandatory crew changes after fairly short hauls. As this process of mediation developed, workers whose jobs were relatively standard in other industries as well as the railroad industry, such as clerk-typists, were able to command wages up to twice as high as those in nonregulated companies. This was perhaps the most destructive of all the acts of government interference. But there was more.

The Interstate Commerce Commission, like most entrenched bureaucracies, desired to effect the least amount of change in the greatest possible amount of time. In order to attempt to cope with the challenges posed by a bloated workforce and increased competition from air and truck, the industry attempted to alter the basic footprint of the rail system through various devices, including abandonment and combinations. These ranged from quite simple and small petitions to abandon unprofitable lines where the traffic had been taken over by trucks to much larger combinations, culminating in the merger of the Pennsylvania Railroad and the New York Central to form the Penn Central. Instead of aiding the process with quiet confirmation or indeed suggestions for minor modifications, the commission did what it could to hinder any change, through extensive hearings where quick action was clearly called for as well as through burdensome conditions which frustrated the intended purpose of the transaction. The most notable of these counterproductive activities was the commission's requirement that the Penn Central include the hopelessly money-losing New Haven as a condition for approving the merger of the Pennsylvania and the New York Central.

These three areas of government interference seemed to me to provide a way to change the court's understandable mindset that the railroads had brought their troubles on themselves. Fortunately, the railroads' own actions provided considerable evidence that they had done what they could to save themselves. In addition to the request for changes they had presented to the ICC, they had attempted a number of innovations. Foremost among them were the TOFC (trailer on flat car) and COFC (container on flat car). This was a procedure designed to integrate rail, truck, and ship transport for almost all goods other than bulk commodities such as grain, ore, and coal. The idea was to fill a truck trailer or container with goods—televisions sets, furniture, refrigerators, or what have you—and drive the trailer or container to a rail head, where it would be loaded on a flat car specially designed for that purpose. The trailer would then be taken by rail to its final destination where it would be picked up by a truck tractor and then delivered to the purchaser or purchasers; or the container could be taken to a port where it would be lifted from its road chassis and loaded onto a container ship which would carry it up or down the coast or take it abroad. The concept proved very successful, but it and other industry advances were not enough to counter the systemic challenges, largely government created or government abetted, which confronted the industry.

The next problem I faced was how to introduce the hopefully mind-altering material to the court, which was why the initial court-ordered round of briefs was a godsend to me. In an effort to confine the case to a matter of market evaluation whereunder it would be our obligation to prove that we could have obtained greater value in sales to other railroads for continued rail service than the government said we would have received as scrap, the court required briefing and argument on two issues: compensable unconstitutional erosion (CUE) and constitutional minimum value (CMV). The first of these (CUE) was an examination of a possible contention on our part that we had been entitled to go out of business and abandon our service obligation far earlier than the date of the actual government takeover—April 1, 1976. The second (CMV) was a consideration of theories of valuation where the court sought to authoritatively eliminate or at least limit the benefit to the public arguments which would have justified obscene prices, such as several billion for the Reading and God knows what for Penn Central. The court treated CUE and CMV as two distinct issues and instituted two successive proceedings to deal with them.

I believed the first issue, the CUE case, was a loser and I spent very little time on it. I followed the lead of the other railroads, particularly Penn Central, and selected a date in 1974, or two years before the date of transfer to Conrail, as a date when the Reading would have been justified in stopping service as a totally losing venture. I supported this with, I thought, a reasonable argument based on portions of the earlier record in the bankruptcy case. Penn Central made a great deal more of this issue, perhaps because so many of its creditors had vociferously and early on demanded a Penn Central shutdown. To no one's real surprise, certainly not mine, the court found that the earliest any of us could have expected to go out of business was the precise date on which the transfer to Conrail had taken place. Hence, there was no unconstitutional erosion.[1]

There was another aspect of the CUE case which I for one didn't focus on to the extent I should have, and which proved extremely important. When the court held that April 1, 1976, was the date on which all of us could have exited the railroad business, one question remained: if we didn't receive compensation in whatever form on that date, were we entitled to interest from that court-determined date until we were actually paid, and if so, at what rate? Fortunately, April 1 was a date of near historically high interest, and the court held that we were indeed entitled to interest from April 1 and that the rate should be set at 8 percent, compounded semiannually. This made an enormous difference in the ultimate payoff, but in my recollection was subject to very little argument and contention.

The second case, constitutional minimum value, I thought provided an ideal opportunity to make my pitch that the government was the villain. I believed that the basic statements of how the railroads in the region had fallen into bankruptcy yet were valuable as acquisitions by profitable lines outside the region would be well handled, as they were, by the other transferors, particularly Penn Central. Instead of simply reiterating what others had written, I decided to devote my brief entirely to the government's destruction of the industry, including the Reading. I made the argument that the real taking had not occurred with the passage of the Rail Act, but rather had happened over a long period of time in the course of many incidents which, though not in themselves cumulatively fatal, destroyed the companies individually and collectively. I commissioned our valuation expert, Isabel Benham, to compile a dossier of cross subsidy, labor interference, and administrative and regulatory intransigence. On her affidavit I built my argument of a long-running pattern of destruction which amounted to a taking. Jim, admirably and ingeniously, found a Supreme Court case (*U.S. v. Dickenson,* 331 U.S. 745 [1947]) which concerned the construction of a dam wherein, as the water backed up against the dam breast, it rose over a considerable period, taking more and more land as it did so. The court in that case held that indeed there had been a gradual taking over time and that the initial condemnation of the land used for the dam breast itself was only the beginning as the rising water affected more and more takings.

Predictably, the government in its reply brief treated my argument with disdain, maintaining that it was laughable that I should hold the government accountable for a series of actions that began in the administration of Teddy Roosevelt.

The court, in its long, carefully reasoned opinion on CMV, rejected all of the transferors' arguments entirely.[2] It dismissed my argument in a footnote, holding, I think somewhat woodenly, that the rising water in *Dickenson* was not comparable to the actions of the government in regulating the rail industry, but also holding quite correctly that its limited jurisdiction was confined to dealing with what happened as a result of the Rail Act. If I thought that Reading had suffered a gradual taking outside the Rail Act, my remedy was to bring a separate action in the Court of Claims.

Then, about halfway through the opinion, its tenor changed dramatically. The court felt that the valuations determined by the government were ludicrously low for this vast and indispensable system of rail, yards, cars, locomotives, ancillary offices, and the complex of other structures, land, and property that constituted the rail system in the Northeast. It pointed out that if it were not possible to determine a fair value by strict market analysis, it might be appropriate to resort to other valuation theories. It clearly would not accept reproduction cost, but suggested that some value based on actual cost might work. However, the formula that it suggested, original cost less depreciation and deterioration (OCLDD), contained clear weaknesses such as adding depreciation and deterioration together since depreciation was supposed to encompass deterioration. Still, applying the formula to Reading on a quick calculation with some adjustments, the number produced was about $220 million, which exceeded my and my clients' hopes let alone our expectations. I felt I had achieved a great victory: I had helped change the attitude of the court from hostility to sympathy.

In addition to my argument which essentially consisted of the unfairness of the government's action toward the railroads over a long period of time, the Penn Central lienholders, led by Louis Craco of Wilkie, Farr and Gallagher, mounted a very strong legal argument based on prior case authority that in a taking of this vast scope, reproduction cost new less depreciation was the appropriate measure of damages. According to a recent biography of Henry Friendly, Lou felt he lost that case.[3] I felt he won. Although the court rejected RCNLD as a determiner of value, still the strength of his argument, I believed, pushed the court to reach for a compromise instead of accepting without question the government's theory of value.

After the CMV opinion, the real work began. It was one thing to secure a receptive hearing from the court, but quite another to prove actual value even on a hypothetical basis. This would obviously be an enormous undertaking, straining our meager resources to the maximum. Before even blocking out the lines of evidence we thought we needed to develop the case, we decided to take the court up on its invitation to settle, using the OCLDD formula as a basis. Without too much effort, we worked up a brief presentation to justify a $230 million calculation. We decided to ask for the $230 million and pitch $200 million as a reasonable compromise settlement. We finally got a meeting date with the government and took the train down from Wilmington to Washington on the Friday before Memorial Day 1977 to arrive at USRA's office by 10:00 AM. There were five of us: Bill Hesse, Lock Fogg, Tom Keyser (the chief financial officer, John Brennan having died of a heart attack at a tragically young age), Drew Lewis, and me. On the way down, Drew was in an ebullient mood. He pointed out to me that this was the way things should be done, since it was basically a business matter that should be settled by businessmen in a businesslike manner. Lawyers might be necessary adjuncts, he said, but they were really pretty peripheral. I had a premonition that things might not work out so easily, but all I did was murmur something to the effect that we shouldn't really expect everything to happen in one day. Nothing would dampen his mood.

We arrived at USRA's office in Washington fifteen minutes before the scheduled time, which was typical of Drew; he always wanted to arrive at meetings early. In due course, we were ushered into a relatively small conference room by a government clerk, anxious, I suppose, to impress us with the government's bare-bones austerity. We were then joined by the government negotiators. Drew proceeded to make what I thought was a very good pitch full of facts, figures, and a well-worked-out conclusion. This took the better part of an hour, which was unusual for a man who always maintained that no meeting should last more than twenty minutes if everyone was adequately prepared. The government representatives, led by Cary Dickinson and Steve Rogers, listened in silence; then they all rose and left the room. They were out a long time. Drew kept asking us as a group, "What do you think they'll come back with? Do you think we're close?" In due course, the negotiators returned; they sat down in absolute silence. Then Cary Dickinson turned to us and said, "We're sorry to take so long, but we had to determine whether we had the authority to say no. We conclude that we do. No." They then got up, shook our hands, and left the room like ducks in a line.

Drew was flabbergasted. "What in God's name was that about? I've never been treated like that in my life." He turned to Lock Fogg. "When are our reservations for?"

"The four."

"Like hell—get us on the next train or get us on a plane."

Well, of course it was the Friday before Memorial Day and the reservations couldn't be changed. Drew glared in frustration. "OK," he said, "I guess we'd better eat."

Looking around, we found a nearby restaurant, and Drew, whom I never before saw drink at lunch, turned toward the group of us and growled, "I guess if we can't work and we can't get out of here, we might as well drink. I'm having martinis." Lunch dragged on intentionally at a very slow but well-lubricated pace. We weren't long into it before Drew turned to me and said, "This is the damnedest jerking-around nonsense I ever experienced. If they didn't want to settle, they could have told us and saved our time and effort in preparation and coming down here. I'll tell you what I want you to do. Howard, first thing Tuesday morning I want you to go into that Judge's—what's his name, Friendly's—office and tell him I won't stand for this. The government has no right to waste my time like this. They think just because they're on the public payroll nobody else's time is worth anything. Just barge in there and tell him that."

I gulped. "You know, Drew, it's not so easy for a lawyer to storm into a judge's chambers without any warning and yell at him. In the long run, it might prove counterproductive. Maybe we should write a letter first so he sort of knows what it's all about."

"OK, write a letter for my signature but be sure it's not long—no legal pussyfooting around."

I waited about ten days, then sent him a draft full of language like "unconscionable," "breach of the fiduciary duty a government owes its citizens," "fraud on the process," and such like. In a day or two I got the phone call I hoped for, to the effect that maybe the letter was a bit too strong and we should soften it a little. I then wrote another draft expressing disappointment that the process suggested and even perhaps mandated by the court should prove so fruitless and be so abruptly terminated. This in essence was the letter actually sent. As I anticipated, I heard nothing further about it from either Drew or the court.

After preliminary skirmishing throughout 1977, we were required under the court's scheduling to produce our case in chief by the end of that year; the government response was due in 1978 with final wrap-up in 1979–1980. The basic theory of our case was not difficult to devise and had really been in place from the beginning. We thought our properties conveyed to Conrail might be divided into three groups: Class A properties, which should have been saleable to a profitable railroad or railroads on the basis of the net freight revenues they could generate; Class B properties, largely used by the lines for commuter passenger service, to be acquired by state or local governments in order to generally enhance the economies of the affected communities; and Class C properties, for which we could hypothesize no buyer for rail use and which therefore would be valued as scrap. Each category of property required an entirely separate valuation theory as well as separate specific witnesses. All these theories together we termed the "alternative scenario," meaning what we argued would have happened if the Rail Act had never been passed and Conrail had not come into existence.

The valuation theory of the Class A properties required an analysis of the rail lines' earning power, what traffic originated on the lines, what traffic terminated on the lines, and what traffic passed over the lines. In addition, we had to estimate opportunity value, which would vary depending on which profitable railroad was the presumptive buyer. We also had to calculate what value we could get for such specific easily transferable property as locomotives (it was generally acknowledged that our locomotive fleet was the best of all the bankrupts'), boxcars, gondolas (used for transporting coal), hopper cars for ore, and other specialty cars, such as those used for refrigerated cargo, chemicals, and the like.

The problem of massively redesigning the railroad with only two people, Bill and Lock, who actually knew anything about the road, was, to say the least, mind-boggling. We hardly knew where to begin. One thing that occurred to me was that now was the time to really start collaborating with the other railroads. I feared that if each of us went our separate ways, our imagined outcome had the Rail Act never been passed or Conrail come into existence would be a mass of contradictions which the government in its presentation would use to destroy us.

The transferors had been meeting on a more or less regular basis, following the urging of the court to cooperate. The meetings in general were formal, addressing procedural matters such as cooperating with the government or engaging court reporters, that is, the employment of a firm that would produce the Special Court reporter which would keep the record of the case: the evidence submitted, the transcripts of discovery depositions and trial examinations, and the orders and opinions of the court. Among the burning questions of the day was that of who should pay for all this. Eventually, after much back and forth, we agreed to a formula of rough approximation based on the size of the railroad and the amount of material submitted, with the government assuming half the costs.

At one such meeting in 1977, I made an impassioned plea for us all to exchange drafts of our preliminary planning and our entire presentations as we developed them, largely to avoid the government's using each presentation against all the others. My primary target of course was Penn Central, which, as the giant among us, understandably had a natural tendency to regard the rest of us as nuisances. It had a monetary stake in the outcome several times larger than all of the smaller estates put together, and alone among us had enough money derived from its nonrailroad assets such as the Park Avenue properties, theme parks, and other investments to present the kind of massive case that could counter the one the government would surely present. Quite naturally, Penn Central's attorneys tended to regard us as basically irrelevant, people whom they were more or less required to deal with but who did nothing so much as interfere with their much more important case.

However, after they thought about it for a while, they realized that we could do considerable harm to their presentation by hypothesizing results, purchases by other roads, or other outcomes which would be incompatible with their presentation. Eventually, at our urging, they came to realize the desirability of a consistent, if not single, presentation. We then began to have much more detailed meetings dealing not with vague constitutional abstractions or practical issues such as paying court reporters, but with potential real-life solutions that might have occurred in the absence of the Rail Act as well as the kind of evidence necessary to support the theories, which to the extent possible would be consistent. This cooperation exceeded my expectations. When it came time for the government to present its evidence against our several cases, there was a large section, probably blacked out in advance of receipt of submittals, entitled "Fundamental Contradictions in the Transferors' Cases." What was remarkable about it was how little there was in it—there were just a few minor inconsistencies which were easily explained or minimized.

As I read it, I could almost physically feel the government's profound disappointment.

Once we had established a basis of cooperation and sharing, each of us turned to our own separate cases. As we looked at the Reading system, we developed different strategies for the Class A, B, and C properties.

The Class A properties would involve somehow analyzing more specifically the component of rail operations outlined above: revenue generated, opportunity costs, and future projection, both for the industry in general and for the Reading particularly, as well as labor costs, labor protection, and a host of other specifics. Obviously, I knew nothing about any of this and really had no time to acquire anything other than a mere superficial knowledge. I depended on Lock and Bill to find the expert witnesses, commission the studies, and build the basic presentation. My role as I saw it was to review what they had prepared, organize it in a way that I could understand, and make it comprehensible to an audience, the court, that was even less knowledgeable that I was.

The Class B properties were those which provided some freight service but were necessary primarily for their commuter service to and from Philadelphia. The basis for valuing these properties was the need to keep the local passenger service. This led to wild speculations running into the billions, ones that assumed that the entire economy of the city and indeed the region would collapse without the service. Clearly, the court would not buy any hyperbolic calculation based on catastrophe averted. We had to determine another theory of valuation.

The Class C properties were those lines which we thought should have been abandoned. These required a totally different valuation technique because essentially they were scrap. There were basically three kinds of assets composing the Class C properties: rail, ties, and roadbed. The rail, depending on its condition, could be either sold to other roads for reuse, sold to a rolling mill to be rerolled and then sold to the railroad industry, or sold to steel mills to be melted down for other steel products. The ties could either be sold for reuse by other roads or used for landscape gardening or other nonrailroad uses. Finally there was the roadbed, which by itself was usually not very valuable.

This, of course, was only a preliminary outline. As the work progressed, the actual evidence needed and where it would come from required extensive analysis which constituted the process described in chapter 8. All we had at the moment was a superstructure. The actual building would follow.

When Reading expanded its workforce to include Bill Dimeling, John Fowler, Stuart Warden, and Jim Frick, Bill and John concentrated on the estate's nonrailroad assets—the sale of Reading's trucking company, a project to sell fill coal from abandoned roadbed, and dealing with creditor groups in reorganization planning—while Jim and Stuart concentrated on the rail assets, including planning for the valuation case. Despite this additional help, our resources were pitifully thin compared with those of the government and Penn Central, where teams of lawyers dealt with an army of analysts, expert witnesses, and consultants on everything from car hire to the effects of inflation to labor production to financial analysis, assuming both the presence and absence of the railroads in the Northeast. Indeed, it proved difficult for us to acquire any independent expert witnesses since all the major players were instantly recruited by either the government or Penn Central. At the outset, I really could not see how we could make anything other than the feeblest case. Fortunately, we had help with all three classes of our property.

As stated above, the government, under the Rail Act, was required to promote competition in the region. This meant that it had to come up with some solution other than a version of Conrail which included all the lines in the Northeast in a single entity. Its response was to assemble most of the profitable lines of the Reading and the Erie together and offer them to the Chessie. The detailed line-by-line analysis of the properties of the two railroads produced by James White's group at Chessie formed the basis of our contention as to the likely outcome of the Class A properties. All it needed was the separation of our lines from Erie's and a little adjustment.

As to the Class B properties, again we were fortunate in that our property complemented similar Penn Central lines which together provided the commuter service to Philadelphia. It seemed to me that all we really had to do was demonstrate that our service was as important as Penn Central's—a relatively easy task, given the fact that each served approximately the same number of passengers. We could then use all of Penn Central's evidence of the public necessity of this service and the willingness of the public to pay premium values to maintain that service for our lines as the mirror image of theirs. I breathed easier as I realized we were relieved of the insupportable burden of starting from scratch in building a case for the value of both the Class A and Class B properties—we could rely on the work of others.

Our problem in valuing the Class C properties was similarly simplified, though not to the same extent. Since all of us were developing nonrail use cases, we all had the same tasks in valuing similar properties such as scrap rail and surplus ties. As an example of the kind of nonrail use testimony we shared, the Lehigh Valley did a small study of the sale of abandoned tunnels in southeastern Pennsylvania for use as mushroom-growing sites, based on a couple of successful sales of their own. We borrowed their argument. Otherwise we might have been faced with a government contention that the tunnels were a liability, not an asset, and we would have been liable for the cost of sealing them.

The real estate, of course, was specific, but I had known from the beginning that we would have to have a detailed real estate valuation of the entire property to demonstrate that the values obtainable for rail use were higher than those for nonrail use, and to provide a valuation in the event the court did not accept the rail use evidence. We knew we had to have a real estate expert value the property but we postponed the selection process. The court wanted to hear the rail use evidence first, and the government or Penn Central had already hired the best-known local real estate firms.

We then had a foundation on which to construct the case. We all knew going into it that there would be changes, modifications, and other issues, but we felt fairly confident about the general direction the case would take. The development of these lines of argument would occupy the bulk of our time in the next four years, and that development, as it unfolded, is the foundation of the rest of this narrative.

6

Fear and Exhaustion

Prior to Reading, my workweek would consist of the normal five days plus a half day on Saturday. I'm not an early person, and would arrive at the office at about nine thirty, intentionally missing the early morning phone calls, which gave me the option of returning only the ones I wanted to. I usually didn't leave until around six, getting home around seven thirty for drinks and dinner with my wife, Maxine (the kids, Rudy and Howard, often ate earlier, though we all ate together on the weekends). I took the usual holidays off: Christmas, Easter, Memorial Day, the Fourth of July, Labor Day, and even Thanksgiving, though for reasons peculiar to my family situation, that one was more a chore than a pleasure, involving two large family meals with too much food and too little real conversation. I was able to take, usually in two segments, about a month of vacation, which mattered more to me than weekends and holidays. Though not the most involved father in the world, I still enjoyed being with my kids, and my wife's company was a constant pleasure.

Vacations were fun. We usually went south to the Caribbean over the kids' spring vacations from school—St. John in the Virgin Islands, Grand Cayman, Jamaica—sometimes returning to the same place, most often trying someplace new. I remember teaching both my sons how to snorkel and helping instruct my older boy in scuba diving while he and I both got our certifications. In summers, we spent long weekends with friends in Nantucket and Little Compton. In the fall, Maxine and I left the kids and took trips mainly to Europe but also to the American West, North Africa, and Asia. Though not much of a churchgoer, I am oddly and variably religious. Ever since I was small, Christmas and Easter have been important to me. I was very content.

All of this changed during the Reading years. I stayed longer and longer at the office, often not getting home until after nine o'clock, which meant that dinner and drinks did not begin until ten. After dinner, I often worked from midnight to two or three in the morning on the work I brought home. My customary half day off on Saturday went, as did Sunday, the only difference being that I worked at home on Sunday. I didn't mind these changes that much; they were bearable. Then, during the last three years from mid-1978 through mid-1981, everything intensified and I minded that a great deal. All my adult life I have depended on vacations: trips to Europe and Asia to visit museums, churches, and temples, to eat high-end restaurant food, to see different landscapes; the Caribbean for diving and swimming; and the mountains in New Hampshire, the far West, and the Alps for hiking and walking. We have never had second homes or boats or other similar adult toys, but have depended on these trips to punctuate our lives, to separate one year from another. When the trips went, I felt moored in a kind of slough that had no boundaries, no beginning, no landscape, and no end but instead an endless sea of mud.

As I got more and more bogged down, I felt increasingly isolated both at home and at work, both of which were affected by my rising fear and general exhaustion. The exhaustion was easy enough to understand, as it was simply the product of the sheer number of hours I had to spend doing the necessary work. What I found particularly tiring were the hours involved in original ideas with no prior guidelines or models, founded upon a mass of details and factoids that had to be organized into some sort of cohesion. I had both to try to soar imaginatively and to concentrate on reams of charts, columns of figures, and computer printouts. The imaginative work was challenging but to some extent fun; the detail work was deadening.

The fear was a bit less self-evident. It was based on the size of the task involved, the huge amount of money at risk, and the opportunity for enormous failure. Even more, what frightened me was not so much the law I practiced as the law I didn't practice. With basically only Jim to help, the list of depositions in other non-Reading-centered proceedings I should have attended grew longer and longer, all set to schedules imposed by the court which were not just tight and demanding but unreal. I was not alone in my concern; even Penn Central, which had a team almost as large as the government's and a budget to match, felt the constraints. I vividly remember a trial conference about halfway through the case when Harris Weinstein, who headed Penn Central's passenger case, got up bravely and stated to the court, "Your Honors, I feel obliged to point out to the court that the pace at which this case is being tried is rapidly approaching a denial of substantive due process."

Judge Friendly replied with a benevolent smile, "Nonsense, Mr. Weinstein. Simply hire more lawyers"—as if any lawyer could be educated in the intricacies of the case in the time allowed before the date of final submission. Referring to himself and his colleagues, he said, "We have been amazed at your ability and indeed the ability of all of you [he beamed broadly over the lot of us] to do wonderful work in the time allotted. Just keep up your great effort."

Harris sank slowly back in his seat with his head in his arms. The desire of the judges to try the case at breakneck speed did not stem primarily from a sadistic wish to exercise judicial power or even to finish the case before their own mortality caught up with them, but rather from a felt obligation to comply with the timetable suggested, if not mandated, by Congress so that Conrail could commence operations free of the possibility that it would be judicially terminated, and also so that the cost to the government in Conrail subsidies and payment to the estates might be determined while the national enthusiasm to preserve the rail system prevailed. Though we all recognized the court's position, that recognition didn't really make us feel any better as we went through the daily grind.

In retrospect, I agree with the view expressed by Louis Crako to Henry Friendly's biographer that Friendly as presiding judge managed the case superbly.[1] In the two CUE and CMV opinions, he narrowed and defined the issues the court would consider. In the schedule he mandated, he forced us all to concentrate on the evidence he thought might lead to a just and justifiable resolution of the case. Without this measure of control, given the novelty of the legal and factual issues involved, the amount of money in controversy, and the temptation to try all possible theories of valuation and alternative solutions lest we be accused by disappointed lienholders and stockholders of committing malpractice for failure to do so, we might well have wandered in speculation to the last syllable of recorded time. In short, he succeeded in herding cats. However, it is one thing to look back in admiration from the distance of thirty-plus years, and quite another to experience the process.

More and more, I felt I was no longer part of a law firm working together with clients toward common objectives. Instead, I saw myself and Jim living in a sort of cocoon, oblivious to everything other than the railroad. I quietly sloughed off my other clients on other lawyers in the hope (which proved false) that I could get back to them after the Reading finally was over. I ignored my administrative duties as head of the Corporate Department in the conviction (which proved accurate) that law firms, at least small to medium-sized law firms, could get along quite well without any administration at all, other than the routine essentials of sending out bills, collecting money, and paying rent and salaries. I remember my colleague Tom Felix, head of our Labor Department, saying, as I passed him in the hall, "Hi, I haven't seen you for a while. Are you doing anything useful or just the Reading?"

"I guess just the Reading," I said. That "just the Reading" rankled. Even at its reduced, ICC-set rate of payment, the railroad had become the firm's largest single client, taking all of Jim's time, virtually all of mine, and odds and ends of others as well, when there were special needs generated by special issues. Also, aside from the reorganization and the valuation case, the railroad spawned many specific cases which were insignificant only when compared to the valuation case. While the Reading was still operating it hit things and people, which led to the inevitable personal and property injury cases. For example, once a ship hit one of our docks, which resulted in an interesting admiralty case that required one of our lawyers to board the vessel from the pilot boat to arrest it before it fled back to Liberia, its country of registry. All of these cases fed others in the office at considerably higher rates than my ICC-controlled fees; still, this cornucopia was "just the Reading." The only person who seemed really concerned about my client was our office manager, who called me regularly. "Howard," he would say, "where's the check?"

"Bob, our bills have to have ICC and court approval and the judge is on a brief vacation."

"OK, but that doesn't meet payroll."

"I've got enough to do handling the case—I'm not a bill collector. Cash flow is your problem; you solve it."

In short, I felt unappreciated and needlessly harassed. I was not alone. I remember coming back from New York after one of the all-lawyer pretrial conferences that took place in either Washington or New York or wherever the court could beg a courtroom, and sitting next to Dave Toomey of Duane Morris and Heckscher who represented the Lehigh Valley. He turned to me and said, "I don't know why I'm doing this—all my firm cares about is the money."

"I know, Dave, I know."

The law, particularly high-intensity litigation, is not only time-consuming and exhausting but also emotionally draining. The commitment you make involves your passions and your whole being, not just your time and legal abilities, so you cannot simply shut your desk drawers, walk out the door, and leave it behind. It stays with you, and a certain level of appreciation from your colleagues as well as from your clients is not only desirable, it's necessary. At the same time, I could understand my partners. What we were doing with the Reading was so outside the normal practice of the firm that it tended to be invisible. It was not one more medical malpractice defense among many or a big real estate deal which involved a lot of people for a short, discrete period of time. Still, that knowledge did not really diminish my sense of loneliness or the fact that there was really no one other than Jim to share the burden. Nor was Jim an ideal sharer. The very nature of our relationship of boss and employee, leader and follower, demanded a sense of distance between us; in short, I thought it wrong to totally dominate his life and counterproductive to express my sense of fear and uncertainty, as I might lose the speed and determination with which he accomplished his assigned tasks if he felt that I had any doubt that what I asked him to do was the right course of action.

There is a long section in the last part of Proust's *Remembrance of Things Past* in which the narrator describes dreams of such intensity that they seem real for a short period after awakening. I had such dreams repeatedly. I dreamt the clear and easy resolutions of the entire case, the tactics and line of argument that would produce certain victory, and awoke with a beaming smile. It was only after five or ten minutes that I realized that that which had seemed so clear, logical, and effective in my dream was total nonsense. There was no way it would have worked. The railroad thus occupied my waking and my sleeping hours.

From age sixteen until very recently, alcohol has been one of my steady companions. It was a source of joy and relaxation, and on occasion led to exuberant, wild outbursts. As the Reading progressed, however, for the first time I felt myself dependent on drink. I almost never got drunk, but I constantly needed its soothing dullness at night to forget for a moment the relentless pressure of what I was doing. I remember returning by train from Washington late one Friday after a grueling two-day session of the government's cross-examination of one of our major witnesses, sitting next to Bill Hesse, and ordering in what I thought was a clear, professional legal voice, "a bubble dourbon." Bill never forgot it, and reminded me of it over and over again through the end of the case. As might be expected, I developed stomach ulcers, and I remember my doctor looking at me wearily and saying, "You know, Howard, four drinks of whiskey a day is not usually recommended as a cure for your condition."

"I know, but I can't help it while this thing is going on. Is there any kind of palliative or nostrum to keep me going?"

"Here, try this," he said, giving me a stomach soother. I am a veteran of all the ones the pharmaceutical industry has produced, from Gelusil and Maalox to Tagamet and Zantac.

I was late coming to tobacco. I never liked cigarettes and didn't start smoking cigars until I was twenty, when I was challenged by one of the two freshmen on the Harvard combination crew I captained to soften our defeat by Yale by smoking a compensatory Upmann Corona. Obviously, pride would not let me wimp out, and I found I loved it. Thereafter, cigars, and later an occasional pipe, became a part of my life. Things changed with the Reading. My pipe smoking began the moment I hit the office and continued all day long, and the number of cigars I smoked

increased to eight a day—driving to work in the morning, home in the afternoon, one after lunch, three after dinner, plus extras during breaks in
the trial testimony. Tobacco is no doubt, as the politically correct never
tire of assuring us, an evil, but it does have some redeeming features.
Among them is that it increases one's ability to do long, concentrated
intellectual work without a break. I do not know how I could have managed the Reading without it.

Neither alcohol nor tobacco nor my sense of isolation at work, nor
all of them together, affected me as much as the impact the Reading had
on my life with my family. The erosion of my private life was gradual.
It took about two years from a time when I enjoyed reasonable work
hours, dinner parties, vacations with my kids, and holidays and leisurely
half-weekends with Maxine to a time when all these disappeared. Not
only did I miss the pleasure I was used to, but I saw myself erode into a
kind of domestic monster. I lost interest in what my sons were doing in
school and in their own growing up at a time, early adolescence, when a
father's presence is supposed to be important. I found myself becoming
more and more laconic. My only real interest was the case, but of course,
this was the last thing I wanted to talk about since the only relief I got
from it was at home. Hence, silence. I remember my wife finally saying
in desperation, "It may be sweet and glorious to die for one's country, but
for a bankrupt railroad? You're crazy."

"Look, I could be fired, which would be great," I said. "I could die,
which no longer seems so awful, but I can't quit. I've taken their nickel.
They can't get anyone else given the schedule governing this case. But I'll
promise you one thing: if by some chance we get through this together,
I'll never, never take on anything like this again. There isn't enough
money or kudos in the world to tempt me. I'd have never taken it on in
the first place if I'd known or suspected what it would involve. Just please
hold out—it will be longer than we hoped, but it won't be forever."

If there was any single factor in my success, it was the courage and
support of my wife. I know it is a cliché to say, "I couldn't have done it
without her," but the reason clichés exist is the simple truth embodied
in them. Certainly this one was true for me.

From my current vantage point, I see another reason I should have
tried (although even now I don't see how) to follow Maxine's advice and

step back from the Reading case. If lawyers provide any useful function, it is the ability to look at the client's problem objectively, to provide some sort of perspective from which to see a problem from the other side and explore where compromise and settlement may be possible. The client who uses his lawyer to do his shouting for him, to be his pit bull, makes a huge mistake, as does the lawyer who permits this to happen. I have seen lawyers identify so deeply with their client's cause that they miss the most effective solution to the difficulty and indeed compromise their own ethics in doing so. The whole purpose of the legal profession is to provide a structure of dispute resolution within the rules and confines of society as opposed to using guns, knives, or rocks in a kind of uncontrolled anarchy. In that sense the rail litigation provides a good model for the separation of powers among the executive, legislative, and judicial branches of government.

7

Detailed Case Preparation

What, then, was the task that now consumed my life—what were the flesh and bone of the argument that I had to make? On the one hand, there was the government's scrap case, with all its discounts and unfavorable adjustments, which led them to offer the sum of $32 million for the entire Reading system, including all its leased lines such as the North Penn. On the other was our argument for value as an operating railroad with respect to the Class A and B properties and as scrap for the Class C properties. I really did not have much hope for the OCLDD valuation of $230 million, as the court had made it fairly plain that this would only serve as a backup in the event that there was no other way to "fairly" value the properties. There existed limited attacks on the government's scrap value, as described earlier, but this wasn't going to get us very far. Therefore, it was necessary to stress the continued valuation argument with respect to the Class A and B properties.

I also engaged in another exercise: How much did we really need? After talking with Bill Dimeling and John Fowler, as well as Bill Hesse and Lock Fogg, about the value of the nonconveyed assets, we came to the tentative conclusion that $96 million, or three times the government offer, would be enough to pay off all the creditors' principal debt plus accrued interest. This, of course, in and of itself was an enormous windfall for the long-term bondholders and creditors who would get their debt repaid on twenty-year 3 and 4 percent obligations in cash at a time when interest rates ranged from 10 to 15 percent. This solution also required the government to pay in cash, not securities.

A recovery of $96 million seemed more or less realistic. It was less than the $230 million that was the maximum we could claim for the Class A and B properties combined. Still, it was three times the government offer, and if cash was substituted for the Conrail securities, it had a value of at least $150 million. In short, it fit comfortably within the parameters between the government's extreme lowball offer and our outrageously high demand.

Almost everyone who has ever prepared a case in litigation has a different way of doing it. Since the rail case was my first trial effort and since it was in many ways different from any other prior trial in that, for one thing, it focused on what would have happened and not on what did happen, I did not seek advice from the more seasoned trial lawyers in the firm. Instead, I began from the back and worked forward. I imagined myself in oral argument demonstrating how the values I claimed were totally irrefutable, even unquestionable. Next, I tried to block out the brief that would support that argument. Finally, I outlined the evidence I would need to justify the brief. The plan became a kind of a schematic or overlay guiding the preparation.

Of course, it was the court that determined the basic structure of the case through a series of pretrial conferences and orders. In order to cope with the variety of possible presentations by six independent railroads on one side and the government on the other, the court, after first considering and rejecting the use of hearing examiners, determined that the entire case would be presented in writing, that neither the court nor any examiner would hear oral testimony, though witnesses would testify orally during depositions. The court based this determination primarily on the fact that the tight timetable mandated by Congress for concluding the case precluded the time-consuming process of multiple oral proceedings. Also, since two of the three judges were appellate judges, they were unused to hearing oral evidence. In any event, the course of action adopted by the court might well have been the only effective way of handling the case and it demonstrated what Lou Crako, I, and others came to believe was the superb ability of the court in handling its almost insurmountable judicial challenge.

It is one thing to theorize generally about how to assemble a case, and quite another to translate those generalities of Class A, B, and C presentation into concrete testimony—in short, to move from general theory or speculation into fact or at least expert opinion based on logically consistent information and projections. Therefore, I was faced with an overriding consideration: what sort of witnesses and evidence could I use to present this case?

The government approached its case in typical government fashion. With no eye on cost, it hired all of the most established transportation experts available (with the exception of Wyer, Dick and Company, which was employed by Penn Central), a raft of investment bankers, and experts on car hire; commissioned inflation projections; and God knows what else. I obviously had to take a different tack for a number of reasons, including the government's monopoly of the available field of experts. Also, of course, I didn't have anything approaching the money required to duplicate the government's case. I was pretty well confined to ex-Reading employees and accountants able to adjust the government's Chessie study. In many instances, particularly with respect to the Class B properties, I was able to use Penn Central's witnesses.

The transferors were ordered to present their evidence in written form early in 1978, with the government being given the opportunity to schedule discovery depositions to determine what the evidence meant, and later trial examinations to challenge it. These sessions consisted of the author of the testimony, supported by his lawyer and other witnesses, being questioned by the examining government lawyer, usually assisted by one or more experts on the subject matter, all sitting in a room in either railroad counsel's office or the offices of the government's lawyers (generally their private counsel, Hogan and Hartson, or Wilmer Cutler and Pickering). The government was ordered to present its counter-rail case in 1979, with the railroads given the same opportunity for discovery and challenge afforded the government. Everyone assumed that the government's case would be largely reactive since its basic contention of the disappearance of the railroads, absent Conrail, had already been put forth in the Final System Plan. Thereafter, toward the end of 1980, each party was given an opportunity to present final rebuttal testimony. The briefs from both parties, ourselves and the government, were due

January 4, 1981, a date which I will remember always. There followed an opportunity in May 1981 for each party to file reply briefs. Finally, in June 1981, there were three days of oral argument scheduled.

In the face of the court's timetable, I began actually preparing the presentation I thought might have a chance of succeeding. This process, though of course it followed the general scheme set forth above, was dramatically different from it in expression and composition. For one thing, it had to meet the patently absurd government contention that the Northeast could do without rail service. For another, it had to take account of the presentations of the other transferors. Further, the transition from theory to fact—such as, for example, what would now happen at a particular interchange—often impacted and modified the theory. There were three distinct lines of argument corresponding to our Class A, B, and C properties. Of these, the Class C properties, the value of the sale of assets for nonrail use, was the easiest. It consisted of Bernie Meltzer's real estate appraisals plus fairly easily obtainable prices for scrap rail, rail cars, ties, and other miscellaneous non–real estate tangible property. The bulk of the presentation in this area would consist of refuting the government's deductions for glut based on the alleged simultaneous liquidation of all the bankrupt railroads. This argument could best be covered not in our direct presentation, but in the cross-examination of the government's witnesses. In any event, under the court's directive to deal first with the presentation of sales for continued rail use, the work could be postponed until after the court ruled on that part of the case.

The Class B properties presented a very different challenge. There, the essence of the case rested on demonstrating not that the properties (consisting of lines committed primarily for passenger service) could make money, but rather their value to the public as a whole and the devastation that would occur were they to disappear. Since I recognized that this case was squarely opposed to the holding of *Boston Chamber of Commerce v. City of Boston* (discussed in chapter 5), I thought an argument based on past practice might be most effective. Rather than rely on theory, I examined what local and state governments actually did when faced with similar transportation disruptions or opportunities for enhancement. Fortunately, I had a good example in my own backyard. In the late 1960s, the city of Philadelphia determined that it needed a rail passenger connection between its airport, which lay some five miles south of the city on the western bank of the Schuylkill River, and the city center. The Reading had an abandoned freight line that was on land adjacent to the airport, which provided an easy connection to Thirtieth Street Station and from there by Penn Central Commuter lines into the heart of the city. The city began condemnation and approval to acquire the property, and eventually did so at a price approximately twice its appraised value for nonrail use. I used that measure of twice appraised nonrail use value as the basic price for all the property I posited the public would acquire.

The Class B property case was also helped, as mentioned above, by the fact that commuter service to Philadelphia was supplied about equally by Reading and Penn Central. Therefore, all I really had to do was demonstrate that the public would do with the Reading lines what it would do with Penn Central's, which meant that I could piggyback on Penn Central's case and let them hire the demographers and economists necessary to establish the inestimable value of rail passenger service to Philadelphia. I would simply sit back and say "Me too." To a considerable extent this worked, since the two systems were complementary rather than competitive. That is to say, together they fully served the commuter needs of Philadelphia without a Reading station located within half a block of a Penn Central station, like the predictable four gas stations on four opposing corners. I raised a few exceptions and made a few contributions to the joint cause, like the example of the previously mentioned line from the airport to the city center, but fundamentally I let Penn Central carry the ball. It was one of the corners I had to cut and that I felt I could cut safely, since by this time I had formed a great deal of respect for the Penn Central lawyers handling their passenger case.

The Class A properties of course presented the greatest challenge and the greatest opportunity. If we were ever going to succeed and get real money from the case it would be because we convinced the court that our contentions regarding Class A were essentially sound. In making this case as outlined previously, the enemy proved my greatest ally. The government, in order to offer some sort of lukewarm rebuttal to the charge that in creating Conrail it had committed the most enormous violation of antitrust laws in history, offered an alternative, a railroad consisting of the Reading and the Erie to compete with a Conrail essentially formed from Penn Central with add-ons from the other bankrupts. They also stripped both Conrail and the new road of the commuter obligation which would have doomed any chance that either might have for success. By this I mean primarily that the commuter authority would become an operator and not a subsidizer. In Philadelphia, SEPTA would own the cars, hire the rail employees, and assume all other financial burdens of the service, including paying trackage fees to the acquirer of the asset properties for the use of its property.

The government offered the new Reading-Erie to the profitable roads operating in the region, particularly the Chesapeake and Ohio (the Chessie). Ultimately, the Chessie declined to bite. The failure of the Chessie, which was the most logical purchaser of our Class A properties, to accept the government's offer posed a real problem for me. I could argue, and indeed planned to argue, that the government's proposed offer was not our Class A properties. It included lines of other railroads and marginally unprofitable lines of roads and excluded lines which we thought would be profitable. Still, this was mere tinkering; it did not really address the nine-hundred-pound gorilla—the Chessie's refusal to buy.

Fortunately, my problem was largely solved for me. After the publication of the government's offer, and the Chessie's study of it, a team of lawyers led by Erie scheduled a long course of depositions, particularly of James White, the leader of the Chessie group. On our side, Lock Fogg attended all of the examinations but the lead was really taken by John Alterie representing the Erie, which was a much larger railroad than the Reading and could afford to devote the lawyers and analysts necessary to probe deeply into the Chessie study. Some months into the examination, John, an excellent lawyer for whom I developed a great deal of respect, made the error every litigator dreads: he asked the wrong question. "Mr. White," he said, "was any consideration ever given to unbundling the package, separating the Reading and the Erie?"

White replied, "Yes there was, and I gotta tell you, John, we thought we could make something of the Reading but the Erie was a dog."

I, of course, made sympathetic noises that the Chessie had under-valued the Erie, in order to keep the solidarity among the bankrupts that I thought was essential to the entire presentation, but a huge weight was lifted from my shoulders. I could now argue that if the government had offered the Reading alone to the Chessie, which it refused to do, the Chessie would have bought us.

We spent the year 1978 building our case on the value of the Class A properties. The principal underpinning of this effort consisted of massaging the Chessie report in such a way as to produce a higher value for the Class A properties than could be realized under the government's configuration and, perhaps even more importantly, updating the calculation to include the year 1974, which was pretty well accepted as the base year in which Reading could have gone out of business under *Brooks-Scanlon* and the year a profitable interest in an acquisition would have been used as the basis for its study. Since this was essentially a numbers game, we hired our regular accountants Peat Marwick to do this work. They performed admirably. Their task was to review the Chessie study, develop rules for translating it for the Class A properties, effect the changes, and explain the end product in words I could understand. My job was to take this product, apply well-recognized valuation principles to it, and transform it into a presentation the judges could understand, with a dollar figure at the end constituting our claim.

There were obviously holes that had to be fixed in order to make the fluffed-up beautified Chessie–Peat Marwick product effective. First, while the study demonstrated the amount of net revenue the Chessie might derive from Class A properties, it did not attempt to estimate the value of those properties to the Chessie, which would constitute the amount the Chessie would likely have paid for them. This was perfectly understandable since the purpose of the original Chessie study was to see whether the offer price fixed by the government was justified or not. In order to transform the study, we employed Isabel Benham, who had an excellent reputation as a financial analyst in the railroad industry. What I did not realize was that most of her experience and her reputation had been earned while working for a senior analyst who had retired. This might explain why our experience with her can perhaps best be described as "mixed," as will be apparent somewhat later. In any event, by applying an analytical method all her own, one somewhat foreign to the value analysis produced by the government's experts or those of our fellow bankrupts, she arrived at a price-earnings multiple that supported a price in the neighborhood of $200 million, which was just fine.

The next problem was competition. The Chessie study, supplemented by Peat Marwick's work, centered exclusively on the Chessie as the presumptive purchaser of Reading. Isabel Benham's work also stated the presumed value of the Reading to Chessie. What was obviously lacking was any sense of competition. If the Chessie were the only purchaser for the properties, it would be very difficult to argue that it would have paid anything more than a very small premium above liquidation value for Reading. At my urgent request, Bill Hesse found a man named Arthur Baylis who, until his retirement, had worked all his life for the New York Central and then Penn Central after the New York Central's merger with the Pennsylvania railroad. He was a joy to work with. He said he felt very confident in opining on the value of the Reading to other railroads since he had competed with Reading-Chessie all his working life. He pointed out the value of its acquisition to the Norfolk Southern or any logical acquirer of the Penn Central system, such as the Union Pacific or the Burlington Northern, based not only on the earnings contribution of the Reading lines but also on the adverse effect that any such acquisition would have on the Chessie system, the so-called opportunity costs. His testimony needed no hints or suggestions on my part to make it fit into the overall presentation, particularly since it used the opportunity costs of another road acquiring the Reading as a factor that would have increased the Chessie's desire to acquire the Reading, and consequently the amount it would have paid to do so.

The effectiveness of Baylis's presentation was demonstrated by the government's response. They hired one John Sullivan, who, in a very short piece of testimony and without giving any reasons, examples, or arguments, simply said he disagreed with Baylis. As I pondered how to handle Sullivan, Jim Frick supplied the perfect answer: "Look, Howard, I've asked around about this guy and discovered he made his reputation embarrassing lawyers on cross-examination, providing misleading and evasive answers in a way that's difficult to counter or control, particularly in an unsupervised deposition."

As we sat there, we both slowly smiled. "OK, Jim," I said. "What if we waive cross-examination and leave the government with this bit of nonsense?"

"Sounds good to me, Howard, particularly since their cross-examination of Arthur failed miserably."

This left the government in its brief spluttering that its witness Mr. Sullivan was unchallenged, which I countered by pointing out that Mr. Sullivan had written nothing worthy of challenging.

With the Chessie–Peat Marwick study, Isabel Benham's valuation analysis, and Arthur Baylis's testimony on competitive offers, I felt our case on the Class A properties was virtually complete. Since I was relying on the Penn Central evidence for the value to the public of the Class B commuter properties and could defer the Class C nonrail value to later, I felt pretty good about our presentation. Now the "fun" began.

8

The Times That Try Men's Souls

The meetings we had of counsel for all the transferors, where we sat around trying to feel each other out, did not occur in a vacuum. Prior to our getting together, the Special Court had made a strong suggestion as to what it did and did not wish to hear, and we had already had the two rounds of briefing and oral argument described above, one on the constitutional minimum value and the other on the unconstitutional erosion. It was clear at this point that if the public remained the buyer, the price it would have paid was limited; perhaps, as the court suggested, it might have paid original cost less depreciation and deterioration (OCLDD), but reconstruction new was out of the question. At any rate, our first line of attack had to be to value the operating properties as an operating profit-making enterprise, not as a public service, or, if valued as a public service, as a key ingredient in an overall rail transportation network. The net result of this conclusion led all but one of us to make up a hypothetical universe in which there were a number of buyers competing for our properties, and, with respect to a public buyer, a number of competitors to provide the service offered by the railroads.

The nature of the meetings we held shifted from efforts to counteract the government's use of each of our suppositions against all the others to something much more specific, with all of us relying on the court's direction to cooperate to get around any accusation of collusion in violation of antitrust laws. For us, the task was relatively easy since we had the Chessie study massaged by Peat Marwick and slightly transformed by our in-house railroad experts, particularly Lock Fogg and Bill Hesse, as well as Arthur Baylis's testimony. The Erie attorneys had a harder time since, given James White's "dog" comment, they couldn't rely on the Chessie study to the extent we did, or at least couldn't posit Chessie as the most logical buyer; still, they were able to suggest a number of acquirers, including the Norfolk Southern and whatever road acquired the Penn Central. The huge Penn Central itself had a great many potential acquirers: all the major roads in the West seeking to form a truly transcontinental railroad, plus the two great Canadian roads, the Canadian National and Canadian Pacific, seeking to expand into the United States.

As we worked together and began to explain the outline of our cases to each other, Stanley Weiss, representing the CNJ, urged us all to stick to the history of what actually happened. This was no surprise, as Stanley thought he had a deal to sell the CNJ to New Jersey for $100 million, which the Rail Act frustrated. Stanley belabored his point ad nauseam at meeting after meeting until one of us pointed out, "Look Stanley, if I had your case I might try it the way you propose, but I don't have your case. I haven't got any good history. I've got to make it up." Thereafter, Stanley stopped trying to persuade us. Unfortunately, his own case rested on the key testimony of a single transportation official of the state of New Jersey with whom he believed he had made his deal. During the trial (which I felt obliged to attend since Reading owned a majority of the stock in the CNJ), the government asked that official, "Did you agree on behalf of the state of New Jersey to buy the CNJ?"

"No," he said, "I didn't have any authority, I didn't have any money, and I didn't know what I was doing in the first place." This exchange illustrates the risk of relying too heavily on one witness, whose memory of events may turn out to be different from yours for whatever reason, including prodding from outside forces. Thereafter, Stanley switched his presentation to value the CNJ property for nonrail use.

The Penn Central, which despite its bankruptcy commanded enormous cash reserves and income from nonrail assets, which Reading did not, was able to suggest a variety of profitable western and eastern roads as potential purchasers for its land. Its principal problem, like ours, was what to do with the albatross of the passenger service.

The Lehigh Valley concentrated on the public necessity of keeping the road in service. Its suggested solution depended on a large amount of public support.

The Erie, while also presupposing possible purchase by western roads, concentrated on demonstrating that it was not a "dog," that the Chessie had misinterpreted the data and grossly underestimated the value of Erie to it. All this, despite the oft-quoted remark of Chessie's CEO: "I bought the Erie once—why the hell should I buy it a second time?"

In all honesty, I never bothered to find out what the Ann Arbor and the Lehigh and Hudson River Railroads' cases were all about. They were too far removed from the Reading's operations to have any real effect on what I was trying to demonstrate.

My own case, as mentioned previously, concentrated on a refinement of the Chessie study, but a prerequisite for any purchase by Chessie, which Chessie made abundantly clear before the passage of the Rail Act, was that Reading be relieved from the passenger obligation in Philadelphia.

The Reading in general serviced the northeastern city wards and suburbs, complemented by lines that went to Conshohocken and Norristown, with its terminal located at Twelfth and Market Streets, Philadelphia. By contrast, Penn Central served the southern and western suburbs along with what was called in the real estate industry the "Main Line," with its terminal at Suburban Station, a four-block walk from our terminal. My job, as I saw it, was to piggyback on Penn Central's case and demonstrate that the public buyer would treat the Reading properties exactly the same as the Penn Central properties. To that end, I assembled a small group of witnesses, largely drawn from Reading's passenger operation, to testify as to this basic equality, and sat back confident that Penn Central would assemble the necessary flotilla of demographic and transportation experts, municipal finance specialists, and others necessary to prove the case that the city of Philadelphia, with help from the state, had both the will and the means to purchase Reading's properties at the price we thought appropriate—about $35 million. Penn Central did not disappoint. Indeed, they assembled a collection of experts ready, willing, and able to demonstrate Philadelphia's eagerness and ability to buy.

As time went on, the passenger case developed a life of its own. One of the many problems in a world of public purchase was that of how the properties were to be organized, and how the trains were actually to run. This suggested to us that the public would have created a terminal railroad, which would manage the properties, schedule the passenger service, and deal with a moderate amount of freight traffic, both originating and terminating in the area, which would run over terminal property tracks, though it would actually be carried by the purchasers of Reading and/or Penn Central, who would in turn pay a trackage fee to the terminals—the reverse of what I originally envisioned, where the passenger authority would pay trackage fees to use the roadway of the acquiring profitable companies. The case for this new railroad (SEPTA) was handled by Mike Clear, a very able lawyer then with Covington & Burling. I briefly glanced at the testimony and projections outlined by Covington for the passenger terminal railroad, attended none of the depositions and trial examinations, and read none of the transcripts, content that I was in good hands with Penn Central's able lawyers. Also, I simply had no time. As the case developed, there were as many as nine depositions and trial examinations being conducted simultaneously, and I knew of no way to divide myself into nine parts, three times as many as all Gaul.

Though, as stated above, I was primarily relying on Penn Central to make the case of the value of these properties to the public, I stumbled across a study by Simpson & Curtin, a well-recognized firm of transportation analysts, which stated that the Reading–Penn Central commuter properties had a value of at least $5 billion to the city of Philadelphia. The study was commissioned by the city in order to justify the expense of providing a commuter rail connection between the Penn Central and Reading lines. I thought that was pretty good stuff. If the public was willing to spend, as they in fact did, some $500 million to construct a connection between the two stations, thus saving the one passenger a year who wanted to go from Chestnut Hill on the Reading line to Media on the Penn Central line the four-block walk, surely they would spend some $70 million to save the entire passenger service of both railroads.

I figured the best way to get this document into evidence was during the cross-examination of the government's witness, Harold Kohn. Harold was a superb litigator whose most conspicuous triumph occurred when he represented the city of Philadelphia and others in a class action antitrust case against Westinghouse and General Electric, based on price fixing, in which he won what at that time was considered a huge verdict. The government in our case offered him as an expert witness as the governor's appointee to SEPTA. In that capacity, he opined in general that there was no desire on the public's part to pay money to keep the commuter train going and that the service wasn't really that important anyway. I assumed, quite correctly, that since Harold was testifying pro bono and only really wanted to vent his anger at his colleagues on the SEPTA board and their counsel, he had not studied the government's case in detail. Tentatively, I offered Harold the Simpson & Curtin study and asked if he agreed with it. He studied it for a few minutes and then in a loud voice proclaimed, "I certainly do not."

"Even though it's authored by the distinguished firm of transportation analysts Simpson & Curtin?"

"Let me tell you about Simpson & Curtin. They're whores. They'll say one thing one day, another the next, depending on who's paying them."

My hunch was correct: Harold had not read the government's passenger case in any detail, if at all. It consisted primarily of a huge study authored by Simpson & Curtin, complete with charts, graphs, and exhibits designed to demonstrate that government purchase of the Reading–Penn Central passenger lines would have been prohibitively expensive and not worth the cost. As Harold continued to expound on the duplicity of Simpson & Curtin, he noticed a strange lack of enthusiasm on the part of the government lawyers and the barely repressed smiles on my face and that of Lou Crako, who represented Penn Central in this instance.

With great litigator instinct, he backtracked and said that Simpson & Curtin weren't really that bad. "My only point," he added, "is that you shouldn't rely so much on experts."

"Including you, Mr. Kohn?"

I went home happy at the end of the day.

Kohn's testimony and the conflicting Simpson & Curtin study really concluded my passenger case. I had enough now, I thought, to write a reasonable brief based on public need, what the public had already spent to maintain the service, and the Penn Central's "expert" evidence. The rest of the work in defending their experts' opinions could be safely left to Penn Central's lawyers.

The real problem of the Reading case was not the public purchase of the passenger lines and the creation of a terminal railroad consisting of the Penn Central and Reading lines. Rather, it was proving the attractiveness of the Class A freight lines to a profitable railroad. The alternatives were grim, should the court reject our rail use argument.

Even though it was obvious that the highest value for the rail properties was as a railroad, I and everyone else on the Reading team thought that it was necessary to prepare for an alternative use. For one thing, the Class C properties for which we could find no viable use in rail transportation had to be valued for nonrail use. Similarly, we had to prepare for the court's rejection of our proposed profitable railroad buyer of our Class A properties and the presumed public buyer of our Class B properties. In short, we needed scrap values for our rail, ties, equipment, and other miscellaneous items, and above all a value for the real estate. The rail ties and equipment were easily valued since there were standard market prices for all of them. The problem with those assets was the government's argument based on glut—all of the bankrupt railroads going out of business at the same time—but there were a number of strategies to counter that. No, the real problem was the real estate.

As discussed earlier, railroad real estate by and large is not an easy asset to dispose of or value. The bulk of it consists of roadbed stretching in a thin corridor designed to connect cities, factories, mines, and markets, which is the reason railroads exist. When originally built, the Reading was obviously designed to go through the cheapest land possible in order to save acquisition costs. Though the total acreage might be vast, its value tends to be small, as highlighted in the previously quoted remarks addressed to our bondholders. That being so, there were some properties—yards, stations, the locomotive shops in Reading, the terminal and headquarter complex in Philadelphia—that obviously had reasonably large contiguous acreage located in areas suitable for other uses, and so had value, although I was fond of reminding the court in illustrating the difference between us and the Penn Central that "the Reading Terminal is our Park Avenue properties."

Despite the uncertainties and the difficulties specific to the real estate, we set about obtaining a nonrail use real estate valuation. We soon discovered that either Penn Central or the government had employed all the better-known real estate firms in Philadelphia to perform their valuation work. For better or worse we turned to Bernard (Bernie) G. Meltzer, a flamboyant real estate broker and dealmaker who was also a local columnist and radio personality, for the assignment. Years passed and from time to time I would call and ask where the study was, only to be told, "We're working on it." Eventually, it appeared in twenty massive volumes. It was impressive, a beautiful job of analyzing our records and detailing our property. It ended with the perfectly satisfactory conclusion that the property was worth about $100 million in gross liquidation value, though without any estimate of the cost of sales or any attempt to deal with the government's contention about discount for glut. There was also one startling omission. I called Bernie and asked, "Where are the comparables, where are the sales of similar properties to justify your conclusions?"

"Oh, I don't deal in comparables. Anybody can dream up so-called comparables. Where I shine is in court. When you get me on the stand I really wow them. You'll be pleased."

"But Bernie, there isn't going to be a stand. This case is being presented as a paper record, by way of depositions and trial examination. I can assure you, you won't 'wow' the government's lawyers. I thought I made that clear."

"Well, I do remember your mentioning something like that, but I sort of let it slip by. I'll get you something by way of comparables if you really want them."

"Yes, Bernie, I do."

I called Bill Hesse in something of a tizzy, expressing my real concern about what Bernie told me, only to have Bill reply, with what I guess he thought passed for reassurance, "Oh, don't worry much about it, Howard. We didn't own most of that property anyhow."

"What do you mean?"

"Well, when the railroad was being built piece by piece through the nineteenth century, we got the property by condemnation. Unlike the

Pennsylvania Railroad, which owned the Pennsylvania legislature and Pennsylvania Supreme Court for most of that time, we didn't have the right to condemn land in fee simple—to get outright ownership. All we were allowed to do was condemn an easement for rail use, which meant that if the property ever ceased to be used for rail purposes, it would revert to the prior owners or their successors. At the time, the people who ran the railroad thought it was a pretty good deal. They paid a little less for the easement than they would have for the fee simple and everyone assumed the easement was as good as a fee since the railroad would go on forever. Now maybe it doesn't look so good. But I think you might be able to argue that at this late date and with the consequent inability in most cases to trace the heirs that what the Reading really got was the equivalent of fee ownership. At any rate, it's worth a try, a challenge to your well-known brilliant legal imagination."

"Thanks Bill—thanks a lot."

I heaved a deep sigh and quickly shoved the Meltzer study to the far side of my office, where it took up one-quarter of the total space. I sat still for a moment, then said out loud, in the presence of no one, "I hope to God our rail use case works." As it turned out, of course, the case did settle on a rail use basis, but I didn't know that when the twenty volumes arrived and sat there staring at me.

9

The Rail Use Case:
Ours and the Government's

It was essentially the transferors' burden to demonstrate the value of their properties in continued rail service. The government's primary contention, by contrast, was that absent Congressional action expressed in the Rail Act, the railroads in the Northeast would simply have disappeared, replaced by trucks on a much expanded highway system, ships on an enhanced intercoastal waterway, increased air freight, and I guess snowshoes. The government believed its role was counterpunching, that is, demonstrating that our contention would not have worked and that our properties would be largely ignored by profitable roads, or at best bought for a pittance no greater than what they would have yielded in liquidation for nonrail use.

My approach of beginning at the end of the case by imagining oral argument had the advantage of focusing my mind and the work product it developed, so that I didn't range over a mass of fact and speculation trying to find the compelling argument emerging from the jumble like weeds sprouting in a yard. Admittedly, it had the disadvantage of limiting inquiry, so that I might well overlook a big piece of evidence which a less structured, more open investigation might have revealed. The truth is, however, I really had no choice, since the timetable set by the court effectively precluded any kind of full-range inquiry given the limited resources available to me and my own physical capacity.

In order to modify and interpret the Chessie study, Bill, Lock, and I then made a list of other areas of evidence we needed in order to flesh out the case and considered who would best serve as witnesses. Wherever possible, we chose former Reading employees, both because they knew the railroad and because we knew them best. One of the few absolute rules of trying a case, as I learned by degrees, is to know your witnesses to the extent possible, know how convincing they are, how they will react on cross-examination. Among others, we chose Edward Lawson to describe what changes in equipment we would use; Stuart Warden, who continued to work for us, to explain the effects of changed traffic patterns; and Jim Frick, who was also part of our postconveyance team, to opine on labor needs, protection of terminated or displaced workers, and revised labor agreements. All proved good and effective witnesses. There were, however, some areas where we could not use our own current or former personnel. As I looked over the broad outline of our presentation, I saw that it was almost entirely Chessie focused, hence our enlistment of Arthur Baylis.

The final witness we needed was someone who would determine a value for the Class A properties. Value in that context started from a basis consisting of NROI, or the income generated by traffic originating, terminating, or carried on the line, plus opportunity costs. From there, the valuation expert needed to develop a value based on price earning multiple adjusted for risk, both macro (such as a general recession) and micro (such as declining traffic specific to the industries and area serviced by the Class A properties). The expert also had to specifically take into account factors that lay between macro and micro, such as a general shift from rail transportation to trucks and planes. In short, everything, including the kitchen sink. The opportunity for free-ranging speculation was glorious. In selecting our witness, we found we were inhibited by the fact that the government early on had employed most of the well-known transportation analysts and experts, such as Simpson & Curtin, and had also scoured Wall Street for the most impressive interpreters, pundits, and authorities (I am trying to avoid the term "bullshitters") it could find—and those whom the government had not corralled, Penn Central had. As a valuations witness, the only real choice who had some credibility but was not working for someone else was Isabel Benham, so we employed her, as discussed in chapter 7. At the time, Charlie Thompson, who represented the North Penn, turned to me and said, "Be careful,

I think she'll give you trouble," thereby winning the Cassandra of the Year award.

Our first responsibility was the preparation of the written testimony. With the exception of Arthur, Isabel, and the accountants from Peat Marwick (Dick Duzak and Jim Gallagher), this involved first outlining what we wanted in a way that hopefully fell a little short of suborning perjury, and then asking the witnesses to write their testimony. After we read what they had written, Bill and Lock reviewed it to see whether it worked with the general overview we had of the function of the properties, and I reviewed it to determine its overall contribution to the argument we were making. Also, some of it required stylistic rewriting, if we wanted anyone other than a railroad technician or railroad accountant to understand it. Lock, who had attended all the Chessie depositions, worked closely with Dick Duzak, and my only involvement there was to try to have Dick write it in a version of "accountingese" that I, and hopefully the court, could minimally understand. It turned out to be a success.

After the testimony was complete, we filed it together with a brief statement outlining our case. The mere filing itself was a project. We lined up a number of trucks that hand-delivered five copies to the court (one for the file, one for each judge, and one extra), five to the government, and one each to our fellow transferors. This meant two trucks departing Philadelphia: one to Washington for the court, the government, and Penn Central, and one to New York and Newark for the Erie, the CNJ, and the Lehigh and Hudson River. We FedExed the Ann Arbor's copy to Michigan.

After the initial filing, the next step was to organize the depositions. Right at the beginning, the whole thing was contentious. Christine Nethesheim, the USRA lawyer assigned primary responsibility for our case, informed me that all the depositions would be held in Washington. I said, "Like hell. They're my witnesses. If you want to talk to them, you can come to Philadelphia, where I'll make them available." This standoff was at length resolved by Howard Wilchins, a USRA supervising lawyer whom I came to like very much, who got us to agree that half the depositions would be in Washington and half in Philadelphia. Eventually, Christine's and my relationship improved.

Once the depositions began, my life became even more difficult, particularly when they took place in Washington. My basic routine was to meet my witness and Reading's backup, usually Lock or Bill, at seven o'clock for breakfast, go to the deposition in USRA's office at nine, which lasted till noon, break for lunch from noon to one thirty, during which I tried to repair the damage of the morning, and return for the afternoon, which went until five o'clock. After five, I went back to the hotel, showered, and went for dinner and a few drinks with the witness and Lock and/or Bill. I was back in my room by nine when the daily transcript arrived. I would then work on it until about one or two o'clock in the morning in preparation for the next day. After getting some sleep, I would get up at six with breakfast at seven and repeat the previous day. Most examinations lasted two days in Washington and some were back to back. As time went on, my initial dislike of Washington evolved into a deep hatred. For me, the city embodied all the evil of Moscow, heavily coated with hypocrisy.

The schedule in Philadelphia was a bit easier since I could go home at night. I also noticed that the government lawyers tended to keep the whole process moving more quickly in the hopes of getting back south as quickly as possible.

I developed a particular technique for these examinations. The material of the testimony was dense and complex, which necessitated complex and compound questions, including leading questions, to which after a while no one bothered to object. This gave me the opportunity to interrupt: "Question of clarification. . . . Are you asking him this or are you asking him that?" In the course of phrasing my questions, I was not above gently suggesting to the witness in which direction I would like him to go.

Understandably, this began to irritate the government's attorneys. "I think the witness understands the question," one would say.

"Perhaps, but I don't"—which was most often perfectly true—"and I think I'm entitled to try to understand what you're asking him." And so it went.

In theory, if in the course of a deposition the parties reached an impasse, the objecting party could call Judge Thomsen, the one district judge on the panel, designated by Judge Friendly as presiding judge to supervise all depositions. The objecting party would then explain the problem, opposing counsel would offer his views, and the judge would rule. In practice, this process was rarely used because of the inordinate amount of time necessary to explain the problem, and because Judge Thomsen appeared to be somewhat erratic. Instead, objections were noted in the record to be resolved as part of the decision-making process.

The examination of Reading personnel went off generally without incident, with the exception of Ed Lawson, who offered testimony on certain necessary engineering adjustments. As we were preparing for his discovery deposition which was to take place in a few days, Ed discovered a fundamental error in his methodology which necessitated a total revision to his submission. Inasmuch as the revision was, according to the Peat Marwick people, something of a step backward, I helped Ed craft it in a way that made it almost completely incomprehensible. We then filed the revised testimony with the court, with copies hand-delivered to the government. The government's attorneys objected loudly, on the basis that it was totally unfair of us to force them to shoot at a moving target—that they had prepared their line of questioning on the basis of our initial filing, and our revisions demanded a whole new line and effectively prevented them from conducting any meaningful examination at all. I countered with the argument that when Lawson was required to swear, as he would be, to tell "the truth, the whole truth, and nothing but the truth," he could not legally be permitted, let alone required, to swear to testimony in which he no longer believed.

The court scheduled a hearing before Judge Thomsen in Baltimore. The judge stated that he had sought the opinion of his fellow court members, Judges Friendly and Wisdom, and that they, particularly Judge Friendly, agreed with me. The argument then became nothing more than a pro forma exercise until, in an effort to drive the last nail into the coffin, I made some concluding remarks, the precise nature of which I thankfully have forgotten. Whereupon Judge Thomsen, the most volatile of the three of them, suddenly took off into a line of inquiry which I thought had little to do with the issue before us but the gist of which was not good for our side. The government's lawyers must also have thought the line irrelevant if not inexplicable, for they did little to exploit the opening given them. Eventually, the judge quieted down, repeated what

Friendly had told him, and ruled in my favor. As we were having lunch afterward, I turned to Jim Sox and said, "You know what I did in there."

"No."

"I damn near snatched defeat from the jaws of victory. I should have kept my big fat mouth shut."

The three non-Reading witnesses brought a different set of problems. The simplest and easiest was Arthur Baylis, whose testimony, and the government's failed response to it, I discussed in chapter 7. The crux of our case, as both we and the government knew, rested on the testimony of Dick Duzak, the Peat Marwick partner who converted the Chessie study into the foundation on which the value of our properties was based. Recognizing the crucial nature of the testimony, the government did not conduct a discovery deposition of him, lest we become alert to its particular interest in what it regarded as weak points in his analysis, but it did schedule two full days of trial examination or cross-examination. Preparing Dick Duzak and his associate Jim Gallagher for trial was a high point of the entire case for me and for Lock Fogg, whose careful examination of the Chessie study was fundamental to Duzak's work. Together, Duzak and Gallagher had every Chessie conclusion broken down to its underlying factual basis, and subjected that basis to analysis and compartmentalization into a workable filing system that made the backup for the testimony instantly retrievable.

What remains in my recollection of the Peat Marwick examination is not the detailed questions and responses, but rather the overall impression. Christine arrived at the appointed hour, accompanied by three unidentified government experts who helped her frame the questions and deal with the responses. When it was time to begin, she leaned forward in her chair, a nice, kind smile on her face, and said, "Now Mr. Duzak, would you be so kind as to explain the assertion you make on page eleven, paragraph three of your testimony as to . . ."

Dick turned to Jim, who immediately dove into one of the six large manila file folders cluttered around him, pulled out the appropriate small neat folder from the hundreds contained in the large manilas, and handed it to Dick. Dick smiled broadly, the sun gleaming on the rim of his wire-rimmed glasses as he turned to Christine. "Counselor," he said, "that's fully explained in work paper 375 (b)(6)."

As the days wore on, Christine's manner of address changed to, "OK, Duzak, let me ask you this." As we broke for lunch on the second day, I heard her rather weakly say to her team, "I think I need a libation." At the end, she looked at me and said, "Howard, I've never seen a witness so well prepared." I thanked her and didn't tell her that all the credit belonged to Dick, Jim Gallagher, and Lock, as I perhaps should have.

My experience with Isabel Benham was different. I am not sure I would have chosen her had I been able, through interviews and analysis, to select from among the entire field of railroad valuation experts, but given the fact, as noted above, that the field had already been picked clean by the government and Penn Central, I was sort of stuck with her. I confess I never really got as close to her as I did to the Reading witnesses and the Peat Marwick pair. For one thing, I never quite understood her valuation method, which was different from the discounted cash flow approach taken by all the other valuation experts. For another, she charged by the hour at a very high rate, so conversations with her were very expensive. Still, I was satisfied with her written testimony and figured that someone as used to giving courtroom testimony as she appeared to be wouldn't be much of a problem. Therefore, I devoted less time to preparing her for cross-examination than I should have.

Her two days of testimony began benignly enough with fairly predictable questions by the government, which she smoothly answered. Toward the end of the first day, as I relaxed, looking forward to a pleasant dinner with Isabel and my team, an early evening, and a good night's sleep, the government lawyer, one of Christine's assistants, asked a dumb, throwaway question: "Ms. Benham, why exactly would the Chessie be interested in the Reading's properties?"

She replied, "Why, I don't think the Chessie would have any interest in them at all."

I confess to blowing my cool, one of the very few times that has happened to me. I faked a coughing fit and asked for a five-minute break, then walked out of the examination room pretending to be totally unperturbed except for my alleged asthma. I went to the water fountain, where Lock followed me pretending to render medical assistance. "You know what she's done, don't you?" I asked him.

"Yeah, she's fucked the whole case."

"Lock, you usually don't talk like that."

"I usually don't feel like this, either."

We walked back casually, hoping to give the impression of total unconcern. The rest of the first day was soon over, with the government surprisingly not seeking to enlarge on its advantage. At the end of the day, after showering and banging my head against the wall for a period of time, I met with Isabel and her assistant in her hotel room before dinner. In as gentle and nonconfrontational a manner as possible, I said, "Isabel, why did you testify that the Chessie wouldn't have any interest in buying the Reading? You must have realized that our whole case is based on the Chessie's purchase of our properties."

"Well, I did testify before the reorganization judge that Chessie wouldn't buy the Reading."

"Yes, but then you were referring to the whole Reading, including the passenger lines and the obligation to provide passenger service as well as redundant lines we posited in our presentation for abandonment."

"Yes, that's true."

"So the properties we posit for purchase by the Chessie are different from the Reading, aren't they?"

"Well, of course that's true."

"And the Chessie might have an interest, as they indicated in their own study, in buying that part of the Reading."

"Oh, yes, I guess they might."

We then went to dinner at a quite fancy Washington restaurant at the bankrupt estate's expense, where I listened respectfully to Isabel recount her many triumphs as a railroad analyst.

The next day, a Friday, was the last day of Isabel's scheduled examination. The government attorneys had some relatively unimportant, unchallenging questions, and they were done in time for an early lunch. In the afternoon, I began my redirect examination. The problem with a redirect is that it often leads to recross, and you end up in worse shape than if you hadn't bothered with redirect at all. Fortunately, I noticed that Christine had brought her tennis racquet with her to the deposition room, strongly suggesting a desire to quit on time. I began with some totally unimportant questions of clarification, and then at a quarter to five I asked, "Ms. Benham, when you testified yesterday to the Chessie's interest in the Reading, were you referring to the Reading as it was before its entry into bankruptcy or the properties we are now offering for purchase?" (Given the technical complexity of the subject matter in general and the difficulty and risk of seeking a ruling from Judge Thomsen, leading questions on direct as well as cross were more the rule than the exception for both sides.)

"The Reading as it was on entry into bankruptcy."

"Then your testimony did not relate to the properties we are now proposing might be purchased."

"That's true."

"No further questions."

The clock struck five. Christine had no questions. We escaped, maybe.

10

The Government's Case

The government's case came in two parts. The first, developed to considerable extent in the Final System Plan, was an argument that the country could, if necessary, do without railroads in the Northeast altogether. We thought this contention patently absurd. Indeed, during his examination, one of the government's key witnesses, Edson L. Tennyson of the Pennsylvania Department of Transportation, blurted out in exasperation, "Who's kidding whom? You simply can't move ore, coal, or grain in the Northeast by land except by rail." We then set about disproving the government's assertion by specific examples.

The second prong of the government's attack was to concede, arguendo, that rail service was indispensable, but to insist that the bankrupt railroads were such hopeless losers that the public, state and local governments and authorities, and the profitable western roads would pay next to nothing for the properties, certainly no more or just a little more than they were worth in liquidation for nonrail use. Their value then would be what the government contended in the Final System Plan. The fundamental thrust of our argument that the government brought the disaster on the railroads was aimed at countering this contention. According to us, if only the government ceased its interference through both regulation and cross-subsidy, the railroads would return to profitability.

The initial approach by the government was to present a number of witnesses (rather fewer than I expected) to defeat our case. Four have remained in my memory: Albert Moon, Richard Murphy, John

Waldron, and James Sullivan (whose testimony I recounted in chapter 7). Together, they illustrated the danger of having too much money to spend. With the exception of Sullivan, they each produced massive and presumably expensive studies which, though impressive in their size, complexity, and obvious careful preparation, were all flawed in their foundation. These witnesses all shared a common characteristic, namely, that they dealt with macroeconomic generalities instead of actually looking at the hopper cars to see if they were rusted through. They dealt with all the railroads together as opposed to each particular road with its special characteristics—what made it attractive to a purchaser, what its defects were, and how those defects could be corrected. Indeed, as I look back now, the entire problem with the northeastern railroads as it developed over many years of government interference stemmed from this refusal to focus on specific needs and market-based solutions in favor of an overreaching view of the nation's transportation grid as if it were a single self-contained entity.

Albert Moon's study was on car hire—the expense of renting cars from other roads to meet peak demand. Shortly after receiving it, Jim Sox came into my office with a woebegone expression. "Howard," he said, "I've read this thing three times and I can't understand a word of it."

"Don't worry about it, Jim—I glanced at it myself long enough to know that it is incomprehensible. I doubt if the government's lawyers understand it. One thing I'm certain of is that the judges, like you and me, won't understand a word of it. I believe Mr. Moon's opus, unlike John Keats's name, is truly 'writ on water.'" I turned out to be prophetic, as in the government's four-thousand-page "brief" there was nary a mention of Albert Moon.

Richard Murphy's some five hundred pages were devoted to the thesis that rising inflation would frighten off any prospective purchasers, since they would see any possible profit disappear as costs escalated. He had graphs, trend charts, algorithms, spreadsheets, and the usual paraphernalia of such presentations. He brought several support people to his cross-examination, and said he anticipated far more than the one day scheduled for his examination. I suspect he anticipated a detailed challenge on my part to both his methods and his conclusion. But I didn't really see the point of fighting him on his own turf. Buried deep in the

Erie's examination of Chessie's study by James White's group, I found
the following exchange between John Alterie, lead attorney for the Erie,
and White:

> ALTERIE: Mr. White, what about inflation?
>
> WHITE: Well John, to tell you the truth, we weren't too concerned with
> inflation. We figured if we ran into inflation we'd simply raise the rates to
> counter it. We assumed if we could demonstrate inflation, the ICC would
> have no problem raising our rates.

I showed this passage to Murphy. "Mr. Murphy, if an acquirer
wouldn't bother about inflation, why is any of your testimony relevant?"

"Of course it's relevant. There are a lot of things going on here—all
these charts."

"But if an acquirer wouldn't consider them, why should we, in setting
valuation for the properties?"

"Of course they have to be considered. They're important." He sort
of spluttered on and seemed in a state of shock.

"Thank you, that's all I have."

The government, taken aback, had no redirect, though it reserved
the right, which I don't think it had, to recall Murphy for supplemental
direct testimony. We left after half an hour, and I had one of my rare free
days.

John Waldron testified that even if the railroads went out of business,
it would not be the end of the world. Other means of transport, particularly trucks and ships, would fill the gap. His testimony was general in
nature, analyzing highway capacity throughout the region and the ability
of ships and barges to penetrate far deeper into the area than they did at
present. Here it seemed best to attack the testimony through one very
specific illustration. At the end of the government's presentation and our
cross, we were afforded the opportunity to file supplemental testimony
in rebuttal. I asked one of our team, Jim Frick, to estimate how the iron
ore which we carried from Port Richmond in Philadelphia, where it was
shipped in ore vessels from its point of origin on Lake Superior, could
be transported by truck to the Bethlehem Steel plant in Bethlehem. We
struck something of a gem. Jim estimated that the average volume of
ore which we shipped over the previous three years to Bethlehem by

rail would require one ore truck leaving Port Richmond every three minutes, twenty-four hours a day, every day of the year. He went on to trace the route of that truck: up Front Street, which tended to have heavy traffic from various warehouses and other shippers of commodities; onto Interstate 95, which is often a parking lot, particularly during morning and evening rush hours; up 95 for twenty-plus miles; and off 95 for twelve miles on two-lane roads winding to Bethlehem—in short, a mess at any time, a total disaster in snow or other inclement weather, day or night or during peak traffic hours.

Fortunately, Judge Friendly's wife grew up in Philadelphia, and he could easily visualize the impossibility of the move. This testimony, plus the remark made by the government's witness Edson Tennyson, effectively demolished Waldron's evidence, particularly if one asked oneself, "If the railroads weren't necessary, then why did the government spend so much time, energy, and money creating Conrail?"

If the government's case as outlined above seems disjointed and no real attack on the Reading case as a whole, it is because it relied on a totally different strategy. The government's attorneys created an entirely new imaginary railroad called CERL (combined Erie, Reading, and Lehigh Valley). They used their army of experts on traffic analysis, inflation, marketing, valuation, labor protection, and the like to demonstrate that this entity could not exist profitably on its own, and therefore would not be an attractive purchase for a profitable railroad.

There were two weaknesses in the government's CERL case, one factual and one tactical. The factual weakness lay in the combination of the three railroads. None of us had suggested that we would either unite and offer ourselves together to a profitable railroad or, alternatively, try to exist as our own entity as opposed to an acquisition by existing profitable roads. While none of us had attempted to make our cases by denigrating our fellow bankrupts, still, for example, there was White's testimony, unsolicited by us, to the effect that Chessie could make something of the Reading while the Erie was a "dog." Also, the Lehigh Valley case rested primarily on the road's necessity to the public rather on than its inherent profitability. In addition, the assumption underlying CERL—that it would be one entity and one potential purchase—ignored the fact that a profitable road might well compete for part of CERL in order to deny it in whole or in part to a profitable competitor.

The second argument, the tactical one, rested on the fact that the government had unlimited resources to try its case, whereas our resources were very limited indeed, confined to the free cash flow each of us had. None of us thought our creditors would allow us to incur first priority debtor-in-possession financing to pursue what many of them believed was a pipe dream, despite some intimidation by the court to the contrary. All through the trial of the case the court had paid lip service to the plight of the smaller estates, which were all of us except Penn Central. However, it pretty well contradicted its previous pronouncements by its schedule, which mandated a large number of depositions and trial examinations at once, acknowledging that those of us with only two or three lawyers (or, in the case of the Lehigh and Hudson River, one) available to try the case might have some difficulty attending, let alone preparing for, ten simultaneous hearings. Despite the wringing of hands, the judges found no way of relieving our plight. Erie decided to give them a chance.

Arguing both the irrelevance of CERL to any case any of us had made and its naked attempt to present us with a challenge we simply didn't have the resources to meet, we moved to strike the entire CERL evidence. Brilliantly led by John Alterie representing the Erie, we mounted a strong case for the elimination of CERL. Somewhat to my surprise and to my great relief, the court granted our motion almost entirely. Though the government in its subsequent briefs kept reiterating that "much of the CERL evidence remains in the case," I never quite understood what it was or how it affected their presentation. I guess it was a sort of otherworldly spirit that only a properly tuned-in medium could reach. I like to think that the judges granted our motion not only because of its nonapplication to the cases we presented and their feeling of moral obligation, but I frankly believe that their primary motivation was to forestall the inevitable requests for extensions of time so that we could prepare to cross-examine the government's witnesses and produce a response of our own based on this entirely new railroad the government had created out of whole cloth. Their ruling demonstrated once again that the motive which drove the court more than anything else was the desire to finish the case in accordance with the 1983 deadline set by Congress in the statute.

I had thought that the period spent cross-examining the government witnesses and attacking their case would be easier than the defense of the Reading witnesses, but somehow it wasn't. This might have been due just to the accumulated fatigue over the previous five years, with more and more of my energy already expended. Or it might have been due to the fear that engulfed me as I realized that there were vast aspects of the government's case I would never have the time to deal with aside from just a quick review of the written presentation. Also, I realized I could not prepare meaningful cross-examinations for most of the witnesses, for even if I had prepared for them, I could not have presented more than a few, given the simultaneous trial examinations. As an example, I left the government's entire passenger case, with the exception of the cross-examination of Harold Kohn, to Penn Central, as I had left most of our direct passenger case to them.

My private life became no better either. I felt myself drifting further and further from my wife and kids and hating the growing separation. I knew I was being terribly unfair to Maxine, demanding dinner way too late at night, losing my sexual desire, and never really being there even when I was there. I grew more distant from Rudy and Howard, and watched while our happy game-playing disappeared and I became a sort of stranger who lived in their house but was not part of their lives.

As I grew more distant from my family, I found myself drawn more closely to Bill and Jim. I felt as if I were the middle member of a multigenerational family, a son to Bill, a father to Jim. I remember long talks on the train with Bill to and from Washington about how he missed his first wife and how he had coped and failed to cope with her protracted death from cancer. Later, he talked of how much joy he had in his second marriage and how hard it was to reconcile his children to their stepmother. "I tried to tell them," he said, "that their mother had made me so happy I couldn't face being alone, and Betty, as my secretary, had shared my pain and was the natural and even inevitable successor, but somehow I never felt it quite stuck." Meanwhile I helped guide Jim in his choice between the law and the priesthood, trying to show him where the law, despite its hardships, could give him a long and fulfilled life. I also tried gently to make him comfortable with himself so he could find a man to love and live with.

As for myself, as my real world, what I truly cared about, receded, I replaced it more and more with a fantasy life. During this time, I took to reading some popular books on astrophysics, not so much for the science as for their sense of how small this planet was and how infinitely insignificant the case that now totally consumed me was with respect to the universe. I needed to feel, at least sometimes, that the whole thing really didn't matter.

11

End Game

In the fall of 1980, as we finished the cross-examination of the government's witnesses, we all turned to writing our briefs, though I, and I think many others, had already started drafting portions of what we wanted to present. Since the court had heard no testimony and had not been given the written evidence, let alone the discovery and cross-examination transcripts, both our cases and the government's consisted entirely of these briefs and the excerpts of evidence each side wanted to present in the form of appendices. Our briefs were due on January 12, 1981, and the government's some six weeks later. In the midst of the frenzied assembly of the summary of six years of intense work which consisted of the careful sifting and organizing of the mass of evidence and forming it so that it told a coherent story, two cataclysmic events occurred.

First, Ronald Reagan was elected president, and Drew told us all that he was quitting as trustee to become secretary of transportation. In short, he was switching from being our leader to leading the opposition. The problems of conflict of interest—of how we could get an unbiased hearing before the court or even the appearance of an unbiased hearing—appalled me. I tried as much as I could, since we were never really intimate, to urge him to take another post. "How about Commerce," I said. "You have an extraordinary record as a business doctor, a fixer of troubled companies. Or how about Treasury—you at least can read a balance sheet, which is more than many of your predecessors could do."

"No, Howard," Drew replied, "my real interest is transportation. There are things in the merchant marine; aviation, including traffic control; rail transportation, particularly selling Conrail and getting the government out of the railroad business, which I want to do. Don't worry about the valuation case. I can insulate myself from all that."

I gave up and wished him luck. In retrospect, the country benefited enormously from his service and the valuation case was basically unaffected.

The second was the announcement in late November that the government and Penn Central had settled their case. There followed a hearing on the approval of the settlement, attended by lawyers for all of the railroads involved in the case, many of their subsidiaries or underliers, and many of their creditors. The hearing was held in the ceremonial federal courtroom in Washington, the only venue large enough to hold it. I happened to sit next to Bob Timpany, trustee of CNJ, who rather sourly remarked, "You know, Howard, I can't hear what the court is saying for the ticking of the lawyers' meters."

"Now, Bob, don't be bitter; we all have to live."

"Live? I never knew bankruptcy would make so many people so rich."

In the course of the hearing, where the settlement of about $1.7 billion was approved (so much for Henry Friendly's opening gambit that those who hoped for billions in recovery would be sorely disappointed), the court took it upon itself to heartily recommend that the rest of us settle as well. Friendly then took dead aim at me by suggesting I settle with Charlie Thompson's clients—the North Penn, the Delaware and Bound Brook, and the PG&N—in the manner Penn Central settled with the Peoria and Eastern. I gulped hard. Obviously, I intended to settle with Charlie's clients in the manner that Penn Central settled with its underliers, but unfortunately the judge had picked the wrong example. The Penn Central owned more than 90 percent of the P&E and could afford to give them what they wanted, as the value of the P&E was miniscule compared with the total value of Penn Central and they were getting their own money back. On the other hand, we did not own virtually all of the North Penn, Delaware and Bound Brook, or PG&N, and their combined value was a big chunk of our total value. I had to adopt another formula for settlement, since I felt I couldn't leave the court's comment unchallenged lest the idea that we would follow the Penn Central–P&E deal be carved in stone on their collective minds, so I blurted out, "But Your Honor, I only have one shirt." This was followed by general hilarity in which the judges joined, thank God.

The loss of Penn Central as a colleague had considerable impact on all the rest of us. Penn Central's lawyers were often annoying, always patronizing, sometimes domineering; still, they gave all of us considerable assistance, though the manner of providing it was at best uncomfortable. I remember going down to Washington for one of our periodic strategy sessions and joining the Erie lawyers who had boarded the train in New York. Harry Silleck, the partner at Mudge Rose who led the Erie case, leaned over the back of his seat and said, "Howard, what are the guys at Covington going to do? I've brought an extra lawyer."

"What difference will that make, Harry?"

"Haven't you noticed—every time they summon us to one of these meetings there are always one more of them in the conference room than the rest of us combined."

"Oh, I don't know, they'll probably bring in somebody from the Estates Department for the occasion."

Sure enough, when we were ushered into the conference room after a longer-than-usual wait in the reception area, there was a young man sitting at the end of the table whom we had never seen before and would never see again.

Despite all the posturing, they did provide important help, so much so that the court directed that they give us the draft portions of their briefs to the extent that they had completed them. For me, their departure was particularly painful since I had planned to rely on what they would say, without ever looking over the testimony they had presented, for the passenger case in Philadelphia. In an effort to build a joint presentation, I had already forwarded my passenger case to Harris Weinstein. In due course, pursuant to the court's instruction, I received a draft from Harris, but it was almost entirely only a reworking of what I had sent him. I concluded that he must have anticipated the settlement. In desperation, I turned to Rich Vitaris, whom we had hired for some emergency help while he waited between his graduation from Rutgers Law School and his induction into the Army Judge Advocate General's Corps, and asked him to analyze the Penn Central Philadelphia passenger evidence and work it in where necessary.

"But what about the government's rebuttal and the attendant depositions?" he asked.

"No time," I said. "The damned thing is due the twelfth of January and it has to be massaged and coordinated with the freight case and Mike Clear's terminable presentation."

"Is this what practicing law is all about?"

"Not often."

At the Penn Central hearing, the court went out of its way to forcefully urge the other principal parties, particularly the government, in addition to the leased lines, to settle. In due course, in early December we were summoned to Washington for our settlement conference. Joe Castle led the group, which consisted of Joe, Bill Hesse, Lock Fogg, John Fowler, and me. I figured that as lawyer in charge I would lead the negotiations, but I was wrong. We were seated at the usual rectangular table across from the government lawyers, politely glaring at each other. As might be predicted, the government had about twice as many representatives as we did: there were lawyers from Justice, lawyers from USRA, lawyers from Transportation, and lawyers from Wilmer Cutler. After a few moments of forced pleasantries, Howard Wilchins of USRA made the offer: $96 million. I heaved a great sigh of relief. At $96 million, they offered us exactly three times their net liquidation value estimate of $32 million, which compared favorably to their offer of 2.7 times the government estimate of Penn Central's net liquidation value, which Penn Central had agreed to, thereby relieving us of the charge that we had settled for too little under government pressure. When added to the nontransferred assets (and the added interest from the date of conveyance), the offer was enough to pay off all the creditors with interest, with maybe a few pennies left over for the stockholders, and it corresponded exactly to the figure I had previously estimated. I saw my life coming back to me—a lovely Christmas with my family, maybe a nice long holiday on a Caribbean beach. Still, it was their first offer and I thought I might jack them up to $100 million, a nice round number which was half our absurd demand.

I was about to open my mouth to begin discussion when suddenly to my right Joe slammed his briefcase shut. "Well, gentlemen," he said, "it's obvious from the ridiculous nature of your so-called offer that you're not serious, and we have nothing to discuss. Good morning." He then got up and led us out of the room like so many ducklings following their mama. I could have killed him. I suppose I have never hated a man more, particularly one of whom I was basically fond. On the station platform waiting for the train I sidled up to Joe. "You know," I said, "ninety-six million plus interest and the other assets pretty well satisfies the claim of our creditors, the people we were charged with representing." John Fowler joined me in gently suggesting the offer was enough.

"Nonsense," said Joe. "There's equity here, we're no longer working for the creditors, we're working for the stockholders, and their offer is just too low to discuss, particularly considering the values you've established in your case."

"But Joe, the case is an argument—it's not a tablet from Mount Sinai. The government will, and the court may, have a very different view of it."

"Look, you've convinced me and I'm sure you'll be able to convince everyone else,"

I simply gave up. On the way back, I sat silently gazing out the train window, and all I could think was, "My God, the damn thing is due on January twelfth, and the court has made it crystal clear that it won't entertain any requests for extensions." My vision of a joyful merry Christmas and a wonderful vacation vanished, replaced by the fear of an enormous effort, like the last push up to the top of Everest when I was already dead exhausted and suffering the lawyer's equivalent of oxygen deprivation.

The reality turned out to be considerably worse than the anticipation. Though the passenger presumed-public-purchaser brief was largely completed, given Rick Vitaris's infusion of the Penn Central evidence, the freight case, with its imagined private acquirer, was largely unwritten. It existed in unfinished bits and pieces: Lock Fogg's analysis of the Chessie deposition; the discussion by Jim Frick and Bob Stewart (an associate working in our Labor Department) of possible labor protection requirements, which would have existed in lieu of the massive gift to the unions contained in the Rail Act (which discussions were drawn largely

from the Penn Central submissions); an overview of the railroad industry at the time the transaction would have taken place; John Ehlinger's
discussion of timing based on the court's unconstitutional-erosion case;
and my own summary of Peat Marwick's and Arthur Baylis's evidence
and Isabel Benham's bizarre valuation theory.

It was now my task to pull all of these pieces together into a finished
product. This involved not only editing the individual entries but also
fashioning them into a coherent narrative, something that at least appeared to be a single story. I felt strongly that a number of the government and Penn Central submissions demonstrated all too clearly that
they consisted of separate essays on different subjects written by different people, loosely joined rather than melded, so that the reader had to
fill in the connecting blanks. I was determined not to follow their lead,
but for better or worse to make the entire thing my own, which meant
a refashioning rather than an editing. There were some unpleasant sur-
prises. I found that neither of my friends Lock Fogg and Bill Hesse could
write worth a damn. Their material had a strong factual foundation and
good analysis, but it lacked an argument; you couldn't see where it was
going. I remember Jim Sox coming to me almost in tears saying he'd read
Bill Hesse's work on necessary bridge and roadbed repair and couldn't
understand it. I replied, "Look Jim, I read that stuff too and I couldn't
understand it, but there are some very astute observations in it. Pull them
out, write them down, and rewrite the entire presentation yourself based
on them. Then give it to me, and I'll finish it."

The longer I have practiced law, the more I have become convinced
that too much legal writing of all sorts—contracts, wills, even briefs and
letters—is haunted by the fear of omission, the worry that some small
point will be forgotten and lead to embarrassment, as well as the absurd
notion that professionalism requires obscurity. The fear of omission is
further enhanced by love of inclusion. I believe the fear is a product of
law school examinations and the bar exam, while the love of inclusion
derives from the drafting process itself. All too many legal documents,
particularly corporate trust and municipal bond indentures, are put together by committees of lawyers, some representing the issuer, some the
underwriters, and some the putative buyers, each of whom wants some
pet language included in the document. It is easier to accept them all than
try and argue for clarity or precision. Also, the larger the instrument, the

more impressive it is on its face and the more justifiable the excessive fees charged for this work appear. In every drafting session I have attended in my fifty years of practice, one of the great lies (modeled on the classic "The check is in the mail") appears, namely, "I have, of course, no pride of authorship." The result is that the purpose of the document is lost in a forest of verbiage which itself is composed of buzzwords and invented technicalities seemingly designed to intimidate rather than elucidate. The end product becomes a mountain of run-on sentences and complex dependent clauses in which meaning is blurred and obscured—sort of like Proust but without any hint of genius in language or imagination. I have tried over the course of my practice to avoid this pitfall at all costs. I may have been dull, but I hope I was at least comprehensible.[1]

I vastly underestimated the time it would take or indeed the real size of the project. What I thought I could handle in a page at most required pages upon pages, even after I stripped away those facts and pieces of information that did not advance the argument, making exceptions only for those inconvenient bits that had to be dealt with if the total product was to have any conviction at all. Otherwise I risked having the court reject the whole thing on the grounds that it was fundamentally dishonest. As the days and nights passed in increasingly frantic reading and writing, January 12 loomed ever larger, like a date of execution.

I will never forget Christmas Day 1980. Christmas is important to our family, perhaps the most important of all the holidays, and over time it had achieved a certain regular pattern. We got up relatively early in time to open stockings and a few key presents before the boys and I set off for ten o'clock Communion while Maxine, who is somewhat less devout, but perhaps more charitable, got stuck preparing for a grand Christmas feast to which my brother and his family and occasionally other guests were invited. When we came back from church, we opened the rest of the presents, partially cleaned up the mess, and prepared for the arrival of the guests. The meal was a fixed tradition modeled on my parents' Christmases: roast turkey, bread stuffing, creamed mushrooms, and frozen peas, with plum pudding and ice cream for dessert. Even the drinks were traditional—my brother and I drank straight rye whiskey from our grandfather's cut glass shot glasses. For the only time in the year we used my family's cut glass champagne coupes as well, and usually one or more of my brother's big kids drank too much and became loud. We lounged about the rest of the afternoon in talk and coffee until it began to get dark, and then the guests went home and we cleaned up in earnest before gnawing on leftovers for supper.

Not 1980. That year, I got up at dawn and went immediately to the library to work on the brief, had breakfast later, glanced at my presents, about which my family had taken special care knowing the pain I was in, mumbled a few words of thanks, and went back to the library, where I chain-smoked Hoyo de Monterrey Rothschild cigars while writing. We did not go to church, did not have my brother's family or anyone else in; instead we imposed ourselves on close friends (I was, in Scottish terms, a "gromley guest"), and returned right after lunch so I could continue working. I had two frightened kids and a frantic wife, and felt like the rotten apple at the bottom of the barrel. Still, I got fifty pages completed.

Somehow, rather against my expectations, the work got done around the second or third of January 1981, and got nicely packaged in its pretty yellow cover together with the 40,000-page appendix containing copies of the documents and testimony cited in the 767-page brief (138 pages for passenger, 629 for freight). At the end, I turned to John Ehlinger, who had reluctantly taken on the task, and asked, "John, has this thing been proofread?"

"Well, sort of. I'm afraid we had better be prepared to file multipage errata by late January."

"Oh, God. I hope they'll take it. I guess all we can do is file and see."

On the twelfth, the flotilla of trucks set forth bearing our briefs, the Lehigh Valley's, the Erie's, the CNJ's, and the Ann Arbor's on the way to Washington (the Lehigh and Hudson River had settled at that point for a not-very-impressive two times the government estimate of its net liquidation value), and, in the other direction, the government's one-thousand-page brief and accompanying one-million-page appendix descended on us. We passed out the government opus among the five of us plus Lock, Bill, and Jim Frick from the Reading. Winnowing the Reading-related material from the rest and reading it at a very slow pace was justified, we thought, as a relief from the torture of the previous several months.

Then in early February we were once again summoned to another settlement conference in Washington. We met as a somewhat smaller group—Bill Hesse, Joe Castle, and I, sitting at the usual rectangular table along with some twenty government lawyers and technical personnel. This time, the offer was $111 million. I confess to having some, perhaps unjustified, feelings of pride, reflecting that this $15 million advance over the "frivolous" offer placed me as an author in more or less the same company as Danielle Steele and John Grisham, though way behind J. K. Rowling. Also, none of the money was mine. I realized that there may well have been other factors that led to the increase, such as pressure from the court; still, at least I hadn't done so badly that the government could with some credibility proclaim that the Reading had no case at all. Once again, I thought that the thing to do was say yes, shake hands, and go home. And once again, Joe took charge of the negotiations and said, in essence, that it wasn't enough. This time, I was only marginally upset, for I realized that I had become a character in a Kafka novel, that this process would go on forever and there would be no end.

We had sat there looking at each other for a while when a round little man named Steven Ailes entered from the back. Ailes was a senior partner at Steptoe and Johnson who, as a quintessential Washington lawyer-lobbyist, had represented the Association of American Railroads, an industry group, and was now the government's lead lawyer charged with effecting settlements of these cases, if possible. He walked down the table, put his hand condescendingly on my shoulder and said, "Well, here's the guy with only one shirt," then turned to Joe and said, "Come on, Joe, let us old Princetonians settle this thing." They walked out of the room together. The rest of us sat and sat and stared at each other. Eventually, Joe came out and took Bill and me into a side room. We sat down and Joe said to us, "OK, the offer's one hundred twenty-one million—what do you think?" As for me, I didn't think. I didn't know about Bill, but I wasn't going to leave that room without a deal. I began by elaborating on the weaknesses of our case, which were many, pointing out that the government could wait forever whereas the rest of us were mortal, and that unlike the creditors, we didn't really owe the stockholders anything since most of them were speculators and arbitrageurs. Then Bill added the final word: "You know, Joe, that with the eight percent compound interest the court has said we are entitled to from conveyance to payment, that really comes to one hundred eighty-six million."

"Well," Joe said, "I still think there may be some juice left in the grapefruit but I guess it's enough. We'll do it." I loved him.

There was another aspect to this settlement which made it really attractive: it was in cash and not "Conrail stock and other securities," which concept had disappeared long ago when this court made it clear to whoever would listen that it was an impossible task to value the rail properties taken and the Conrail stock given in exchange, particularly when Conrail early on gave no sign of ever becoming profitable. Also gone were the "certificates of value" which were supposed to fill any shortfall in value between the cash value of the rail assets and the Conrail securities. We did not have to explain to the widow of some guy killed in a railroad accident, "Here's this nice certificate for Conrail stock plus this lovely piece of government paper that says it might be worth something someday."

There followed the usual round of cheer and good humor as we all shook hands, smiled, and congratulated each other. The government representatives then explained that although they had the power to negotiate a deal, it had to have the approval not only of USRA, for whom they could speak, but also Transportation, Justice, Treasury, and the Office of Management and Budget, and that they would undertake to obtain those clearances, but it might take some time. In the meantime, it was vital that the entire settlement be kept secret. Neither we nor they were authorized to talk about it to anyone. Obviously, this injunction was far too broad. They had to describe the settlement proposal in some detail to their colleagues in Transportation, Justice, Treasury, and Budget, and Joe and I had to explain it to the Reading management who had succeeded the trustees on January 1, 1981, as the final event in implementing the plan of reorganization. Still, all of us took what we thought were necessary steps to protect the deal's secrecy. I spectacularly failed.

I was returning to my office at about 5:00 PM some ten days after the settlement when Bill Hesse waylaid me on the ground floor of the Packard Building where we had our offices.

"Howard, have you seen today's *Evening Bulletin*?"

"Of course not, Bill, I haven't had time to read local papers for quite a while now."

"Well, I think you'd better read this, and I don't think you'll like it."

There on the front page of the business section was an interview with Bill Dimeling by Peter Binzen, the paper's principal business columnist, who had written a very good book called *The Wreck of the Penn Central* on that railroad's decline and fall and was now focusing on the Reading and our plans for the future. After Bill described, in a general way, his ideas about business investment and expansion using our net operating loss carry forward, Peter asked the obvious question: How was Reading going to fund all this and meet its debt repayment obligations under the plan? Bill casually replied that this would be taken care of through the $121 million settlement Reading had just made with the government.

I felt rather as I did when Isabel Benham testified that the Chessie wouldn't have any interest in the Reading. I stood there stupefied for a time, then said to Bill, "It's after five—don't you think those government lawyers will have gone home and this can wait till tomorrow?"

"I don't know—they're pretty hardworking, and we can't afford to have them find out about this indirectly if, say, a wire service picks it up."

Reluctantly, I agreed with him, so I went up to my office and placed a call to Steve Rogers and Cary Dickenson. Unfortunately, they were both there. After I explained about the article, I could put the receiver down since I could hear them yelling from across the Potomac to Philadelphia without benefit of electronic assistance. In a while, they calmed down a bit and insisted, quite rightly, that it was my duty to explain this entire mess to the court. I spent all the next day writing one of the more difficult letters of my life. After summarizing very briefly the negotiations and then the tentative settlement reached, I stated that the government had insisted in no uncertain terms that the entire matter was to be kept confidential, and that although neither I nor, I believed, anyone in my firm had broken that commitment, I had failed to "exercise that degree of control over my client that the court had every right to expect." With characteristic good sense and grace, none of the judges acknowledged my letter, though many months later, in their opinion summarizing the valuation case and the settlements achieved, they briefly commented that they had had some advance notice of the Reading settlement.

Despite the security breach, the approval process on the part of the government at first proceeded much more quickly than I thought it would. We had no trouble getting approvals from Transportation (where, of course, Drew recused himself, though I think no one had any doubts as to his views), Justice, and Treasury. From there, it went to Budget, and there it stuck.

As the government—in the person of a Steptoe and Johnson partner named John Labovitz—explained it to me, David Stockman, director of Budget, saw no reason to pay "now in cash," an obligation which could instead be deferred for a number of years, perhaps beyond Reagan's reelection. John said he promised to change Stockman's mind by convincing him that the discount from the $200 million for the Class A properties and the $35 million from the public payment for the passenger service that we argued for had more or less justified the current-payment premium stipulated in the settlement. I inquired about when he thought this could be done, and he replied he hadn't a clue.

"OK, John," I said, "that leaves me with the task of preparing a reply brief due in April and an oral argument at the end of May for a case that's settled. How do I explain to my clients, the new Reading management, why they have to pay huge legal bills for a case that's over?"

"Well, Howard, Stockman is my problem—your clients are yours."

Of all the frustrations I had in dealing with the government, this failure of the director of Budget to see what was really involved in this case was perhaps the most annoying. After disposing of 90 percent of the problem in approving the Penn Central settlement, his failure to realize that the small additional payment to Reading, and probably later to Erie, Lehigh Valley, Ann Arbor, and CNJ, amounted to very little in the total annual budget. On the other hand, failure to approve the settlement because of some slight political expediency jeopardized the sale of Conrail to the public by way of an initial public offering (IPO) and the exit of the government from the railroad business, which was an important part of the Reagan railroad and economic policy. Such failure, too, would have enraged the court and could have led to enormous judgments in favor of the railroads. It also would have destroyed the timetable established by Congress in the Rail Act, which might have led to other unanticipated problems. In short, it was plain dumb.

Predictably, as the bills came out month after month, the guys from Chicago became increasingly upset. All I could do was say that it was necessary insurance: if the settlement broke down, we couldn't afford to be in court with an incomplete or half-assed presentation. Reluctantly and dead tired, Jim and I, with help from John Ehlinger, Bob Stewart, Rich Vitaris, Lock, Bill, and the others corralled into the project, began drafting the reply. At this point, the writing became a bit strange. I quoted the line "imitate the action of the tiger" from Shakespeare's *Henry V;* Jim referenced the Gospel according to St. John—material that was usually absent from legal briefs. Bill Hesse, deploring the lack of professionalism in our treatment, was mildly appalled by this. I responded, "Look, Bill, we all need something light and fun to get us through this drudgery; cut us some slack." The government, too, was not immune to flights of fancy. In the midst of its reply was a fairly long playlet entitled "The World according to Erie," which attempted a satire of the Erie case.

The real task of the reply brief, once we got into it, was not all that difficult. Once the CERL evidence had been rejected by the court, the government's initial brief consisted of criticisms of what it thought our position might be. In essence, it rejected the entire notion of the feasibility of a rail use scenario other than Conrail, which meant the brief was directed to criticizing our contentions rather than advancing theories of its own. It is considerably easier to criticize a criticism than to refute a new concept. In a last-ditch attempt to avoid having to file and continue through oral argument, I called John Labovitz, told him that I was about to file a singularly nasty and abusive reply brief, and asked him if there was any hope that the settlement might go through. His answer was simply, "We're working on it."

The court set the dates of June 5 to 7, 1981, for oral argument, which coincidently corresponded to my twenty-fifth college reunion. For a fleeting moment, I thought of attending the reunion and saying the hell with the whole railroad nonsense, but there are less messy and more becoming ways of committing suicide.

My enthusiasm for the continued fight was considerably dampened when I thought about whom I was fighting for. The usual posture of those who crusade against giant institutions such as the federal government is to represent themselves as champions of the poor, the oppressed, and the downtrodden. I had sort of a problem with that. The Chessie, in an effort to protect itself from the colossus of the Penn Central, built up a rival network, buying 51 percent of the Reading stock, which in turn owned 51 percent of the Central Railroad of New Jersey, thereby creating an entity large enough to present some sort of challenge to Penn Central. The Chessie, having rejected the government's overtures to acquire full ownership of the Reading and the Erie as a competitor to Conrail, was anxious to sell its Reading stock, particularly since in 1974 it appeared that the Reading stock had no value whatever and even the secured creditors would be lucky to get fifty cents on the dollar for their claims. Also, the Chessie needed a capital loss to balance some gains on asset sales they had made. Coincidentally, a group of four friends—John Mabie, Lee Cotton, Tom Reynolds, and John Sullivan—were at a cocktail party in one of their houses in Chicago. After a few beers or whatnot, one of them said, "You know, I've always wanted to own a railroad, ever since I was a kid." Another, I believe Tom Reynolds, said, "I understand the Chessie needs a capital loss and might sell its worthless stock in the Reading. Let's offer them a pittance."

They ponied up twenty-four thousand dollars, or six thousand apiece, acquired Chessie's 51 percent of the Reading, and thus became poster boys for the government's case as examples of who exactly would profit from large awards in the valuation case. I, of course, countered that the question of who actually got the money was irrelevant to the issue of how much the Reading was worth. After all, the actual ownership of the company could and did change on a daily basis as bonds and stock were sold and bought. Still, the impression left with the court was less than ideal.

Although the reorganization was complete as of January 1, 1981, and John Sullivan became president and CEO of the company, he left all decisions with respect to the case to Joe Castle, who had made the deal. This was a great blessing to me, since I thought of Joe as a good friend whom I felt I knew well after our years of working together. It would have been difficult for me at this point to interface with someone whom I hardly knew.

It was with resigned reluctance, then, that I boarded the train to Washington together with Jim Sox, Lock, and Bob Stewart (who was there for the labor protection part of the argument). My sense of well-being did not improve as we settled in at the hotel and added the final touches to the argument I was to present the next day. Since I presumably had settled out, I yielded half my time to the Erie, Lehigh Valley, and CNJ, so my problem was how to fit the most important points into the half hour left me. I worked with Lock and Bob for an hour or so before dinner, then afterward sat down with Jim to cover the crux of the rail use argument and try to anticipate the court's questions. After about two hours, we were pretty well done, but I desperately didn't want to be alone. All of the days and years I had spent seemed to weigh on me like a rock. After a long silence Jim said, "Well if that's it I think I'll go back to my room and get some sleep."

"Yeah, good night, Jim."

I got undressed, crawled into bed, and lay sleepless for five hours before it was time to get up, have breakfast, and go to court. I was flat. No, strike that—I was awful. I made the points we had worked out, but did so in a listless, unconvincing manner, and fielded the court's (Judge Friendly's) questions badly. At one point, when asked, "You can't go to Philadelphia from Reading on the Reading, can you?" I equivocated, instead of saying, "Of course you can, it's the main line," which was true. There was something in the way he asked the question that made me think I had missed a fundamental point. I suppose if he had asked, "You aren't really Howard Lewis, are you?" I would have replied, "Of course, I'm not."

The second day was the government's turn. There was nothing particularly surprising in their presentation. Since they, like me, still anticipated a settlement with Reading, they concentrated their fire on the Erie and to a lesser extent the Lehigh Valley and the CNJ, although there was one dig at me that rather annoyed me. They made much of the fact that in the passenger case I had relied to a considerable extent on Penn Central's witnesses even though I had not "bothered" to attend the government's depositions of those witnesses, suggesting, I suppose, that I had been warming myself on some Caribbean beach while the examinations took place. As mentioned before, throughout the case the court paid lip service to the plight of the "smaller" estates because of our inability to mount a 40- or 50-lawyer team like the one assembled by Penn Central, let alone the 175 lawyers who signed one or more of the government's filings. However, the supposed sympathy produced very little in the way of actual relief or consideration, other than the striking of the CERL fantasy. In a proceeding with a staggering number of simultaneous depositions, all of which I should have attended, there was not a whole lot of time for lying on Caribbean beaches. My first instinct was to nail the government's unfairness and lack of understanding during the reply period allotted us the day after the government argument, but then I decided that was self-indulgent; there were more important matters to take up than assuaging my sense of personal offense.

The morning of the third day was relatively uneventful. I corrected my confusion about Reading's line to Philadelphia and pointed out a few obvious but relatively unimportant mistakes made by the government, but generally I simply sat back and listened to my fellow lawyers for the other estates. The afternoon was rather more interesting. The court did not allow the government to say more than ten words before it began to complain, through a series of questions, that there had been no further settlements after Penn Central other than the Lehigh and Hudson River. The court, looking pointedly at me, suggested strongly that the government might try extra hard to be more reasonable and that there were some fairly huge numbers floating around that when viewed through rose-colored glasses might not be totally inconceivable. Bill Perlik, for the government, assured the court that they were working full time to reach an agreement. I, of course, couldn't have been more pleased. The court had given the negotiators the ammunition necessary to move even the Budget office forward. As Bob Stewart kindly drove me home after we checked out of the hotel, for the first time in five years I couldn't think of half a dozen things that had to be done yesterday. I returned to my wife and kids as an almost human being.

The next few weeks were peculiar. On the one hand, the Reading was largely in abeyance and I could devote, without compelling pressure, some time to the remnants of my practice that still existed. On the other, I lived primarily in constant anticipation of some news from Washington, which made it difficult to concentrate on anything else. I felt like a prisoner awaiting the results of his appeal, absorbed in daily tasks that had no real meaning. In early July, the logjam broke and I got a call from John telling me that Budget had relented, under mounting pressure from everyone else, and we had a deal. While this did not mean that everything was over and all we had to do was sit back and wait for a check to come in the mail, it did mean that we could move forward in a new direction: the transformation of the deal from a one-sentence "I'll pay you one hundred twenty-one million, plus interest" into an elaborate settlement agreement.

The principal problem in working out the settlement was one of allocation, that is, how to divide the proceeds among the Reading itself and its various constituent parts, principally the North Penn, the East Penn, the PG&N, and the Delaware and Bound Brook, all of which after all were separate entities with separate management, creditors, and shareholders. Fortunately, in computing its estimate of net liquidation value, the government had already broken down its estimate of Reading's value into those parts, recognizing that each was an independent entity. We then decided to adopt the formula that Penn Central had used in determining what it would offer to us for our 50 percent interest in the Pennsylvania Reading Seashore Lines. Under that formula, we computed the amount by which the settlement offer for the entire system exceeded the determination of net liquidation value for the system (in our case 400 percent), then applied that as a multiplier to the net liquidation value of the constituent entities such as the Delaware and Bound Brook, and to that we added 10 percent as a premium.

All of the underliers, except the North Penn, tentatively agreed to our proposal on the condition that we didn't offer more favorable terms to any of the others. In short, we had to bring them all in or we wouldn't have any of them. This meant a fight with the North Penn. During the long course of the trial, I became less and less fond of the people from Oppenheimer and Company who had bought out the old ladies and trust officers and owned a controlling interest in the North Penn. The word "pigs" kept coming to mind whenever I thought of them.

Among other things, they fired their lawyer, Charlie Thompson, with whom I had established a good working relationship, after they first insisted that he give up the Delaware and Bound Brook on the basis of a theoretical, but practically far-fetched, conflict of interest. Therefore, I wasn't very surprised that at the hearing held to approve the government-Reading settlement only the North Penn's attorney objected. He had some absurdly inflated value based on the volume of traffic passing over their lines, refusing to recognize that origin and destination are more important factors in valuing rail service than passage is. The traffic can almost always be routed over a variety of other or competing lines, or internally over other lines of the same road.

The North Penn lawyer kept emphasizing his inability to understand our valuation as there were not enough traffic-density studies. Over and over, he kept repeating, "We don't know how they did it." After about fifteen minutes of this, Judge Friendly interrupted: "But they've told you exactly how they did it. They took the government's liquidation value, applied the government's offered multiple of four to it, then added ten percent. It may not be very scientific, but there's nothing about it that offends the conscience." At the end of the day the court had signed the order approving the settlement and we could go forward.

Going forward, however, still left the problem of what to do about the North Penn. I favored cutting them out of the deal altogether in the certain conviction that they lacked the resources—human and financial—as well as the five years of background to successfully litigate their own valuation case against the government, and that in time, after wasting a great deal of effort and money, they would accept what we had negotiated for them with their tail between their legs. Joe, who occasionally took a more sensible view of things, suggested that failure to settle with the North Penn, even if it didn't screw up the entire deal, at the least would delay and complicate it, and that maybe we should find some sort of accommodation.

"You mean a bribe."

"Not exactly, but some sort of arrangement."

"Joe, I can't give them more than we offered all the other underliers. I've given my word. Also, the other roads might well have grounds to petition the court to vacate the settlement, which would leave us looking pretty ugly both to them and to the government as well as infuriate the court."

"You know," Joe said, "the North Penn owns some nice real estate that wasn't conveyed to Conrail. We could buy it, combine it with some of our nonrail assets, and maybe sell it at a profit."

"You mean we should overpay for their land so Pat Cestaro of Oppenheimer can make a nice fat bonus."

"Sometimes you're so crude. Look, real estate values are largely sub-jective. What looks inflated to one person is a bargain to someone else."

"OK. It's your call."

We did in fact buy the North Penn real estate at values I could live with (barely), without challenge. The North Penn withdrew its objec-tions, and Cestaro got his bonus.

That summer, I got a two-week vacation. That summer, I got a two-week vacation (the repetition is intentional), the first in three years. Max-ine and I parked the kids in camp and went unadventurously to France, where we rented a car and lazed up and down the Loire Valley, drinking and eating at the high end of the hog. We spent a lot of time in each other's arms as layer after layer of stress peeled away from me.

The rest of the summer I spent working out an elaborate agreement detailing the structure of the settlement of the case and when and to which Reading entity payment would be made. The agreement was writ-ten by the Wilmer Cutler office on behalf of the government and in page after page, unnecessarily I felt, charted the course of when and where and under what circumstances the government would affect payment. Granted, there were a few minor details to clear up. Prominent among them was the Allentown Terminal Railroad, which was owned jointly by the Reading and the CNJ. The CNJ believed that the values we accepted for that piece of road were grossly inadequate, which left the government in a quandary when a case that they thought they had settled proved not to be fully settled. I solved that one fairly easily by saying, "We'll take payment for our fifty percent of the Allentown Terminal at the rate we negotiated—what you do with the CNJ to resolve the other fifty percent is up to you and them." That worked.

The Allentown problem was generally illustrative of what I and the lawyer from Wilmer did over the course of the summer. This gentle-manly discourse was totally different from the frenzied and head-to-head adversarial confrontation which characterized the case as a whole. There were, in fact, times when we could engage in friendly bullshit. I remem-ber his saying to me, "Aren't you worried about what you're going to do now that this is over? But I suppose you're high-enough up in your firm that your partners will take care of you."

"Are you kidding? You don't know my firm. [These words turned out to be prophetic.] No, I've done a certain amount of self-protection. While, of course, I couldn't buy any Reading stock or bonds, I saw no reason why I couldn't buy Penn Central securities. I knew nothing about their reorganization except what I read in their court filings, which were available to everyone. From this, I recognized two things about the Penn Central reorganization. First, they didn't have time to fight about which of their innumerable bond issues was more valuable than the others; second, they were listening to the same vibes I was, to the effect that the court wasn't buying your ridiculous scrap value theory. Given that reasoning, I bought a lot of the New York Central refunding and rehabilitation bonds, which were the least well-secured of all their issues and hence the cheapest. In fact, I paid between four and five dollars per hundred dollars and it looks as if they will pay off under the Penn Central settlement and the reorganization based on it at one hundred twenty."

"Shit. I bet those bastards at Covington were busy buying Reading bonds. We couldn't buy anything."

Another memory from early that summer involves the formal meeting I had in the Wilmer Cutler office of Bill Perlik, leader of the government team, where the two of us signed the settlement agreement. After some polite chitchat, Bill said, "I suppose, like me, you can now turn to that backlog of cases you have put off while you tried this monster."

"Well, actually, Bill, no. There isn't any backlog. I'm basically a business and estates lawyer."

He looked at me rather like an NBA coach whose team had just lost to the St. Margaret's girls' basketball varsity. He graciously offered lunch. I declined, based on an all-too-real cold and a strong desire to leave Washington for home as quickly as possible. He seemed relieved.

On October 1, the first installment of $100 million became due. Bill Hesse and I went down to Washington to be sure that the payment, which constituted the bulk of the money owed us, went through without a hitch. We convened at a quarter past nine in a small conference room in the Wilmer office—Bill and I, a guy from Treasury, and one of Wilmer's Business Department lawyers. We cleared up the paperwork in fairly short order, and the Treasury official made a phone call and determined that the money had left the government by wire to Reading's account at

the First Pennsylvania Bank at nine o'clock that morning. We sat back
and relaxed, awaiting confirmation of the money's arrival, which we expected any moment from Tom Keiser, still our first financial officer. We
chatted away about the local baseball and football teams, about which
I knew nothing and cared less, the weather, and various other pieces of
small talk. From time to time Bill would call Tom, who reported he had
heard nothing, and the man from Treasury would call home base and be
reassured that the money was long gone. We then sat in stony silence as
the minutes and hours dragged on. For us, time was of some importance
since the Reading had bought repos which would lose a day's interest (at
a time when a day's interest on $100 million was actually worth some-
thing) if payment weren't made by one o'clock that afternoon.

Finally, at a quarter to one, Tom called, and in his cheerful what-
me-worry voice told us that we got the money and that actually the government had made a mistake and wired us twenty thousand dollars too
much. The man from Treasury turned green and blurted out, "Of course,
you'll reverse the transaction."

Bill and I with one voice replied, "Like hell we will. We'll do our
best to wire you back the overage as quickly as possible, but we are not
reversing the transaction." I wasn't sure whether our decision exposed
us to criminal liability; all I knew was that after five years of intense
struggle to get some semblance of just compensation, we were not going
to reverse that transaction. As it turned out, we got the twenty thousand
back to Treasury almost instantaneously and everyone left happy. Some
years later, I asked a prominent banker how a money wire could leave
Washington at nine and not get to Philadelphia till a quarter to one. His
response was, "Oh, it happens all the time. The guys in the wire room
were probably sitting around playing poker or playing with themselves.
It's normal procedure."

As soon as possible after the burst of euphoria following the news
of the money's successful arrival in Philadelphia, I left for the airport
to fly, faster than the money, to Philadelphia, change planes, and take a
commuter flight to Atlantic City where our firm was holding its annual
retreat. On the plane, I bathed in a false glow of personal satisfaction,
thinking that I had been responsible for winning the largest case that
office ever had. I had visions of laurel wreaths and fatted calves amid a

euphoria of welcome-backs and effusive congratulations. I disembarked from the plane, checked into the hotel, and joined my partners listening to a presentation by my fellow partner Walter Milbourne on strategic planning or some such thing. The thrust of Walter's argument centered on the weakness of our Corporate Department and my deficiencies as its leader, considering the Corporate Department was one of the few profit centers of the firm, as opposed to Walter, who was clearly a nonprofit center. After all, he said, we were not general counsel for IBM or General Motors or even General Electric, though why a medium-sized Philadelphia law firm should be general counsel for any member of that group of giant multinational corporations seemed to have escaped him. What was really at issue was that the big case was over and my percentage was vulnerable. Indeed, when it came to the year-end division of the spoils, I found my take reduced by five thousand dollars, and oddly enough, Walter's increased by the same amount.

Needless to say, I was devastated. Where I had expected an outpouring of congratulations, I found only Tom and Grant to say how much they appreciated what I had done. I drank heavily, and at the end of a torturous dinner turned to Tom and said, "For Christ's sake, get me the hell out of here." He took me to one of the casinos—I think Bally's but I can't be sure—and plunked me down in front of a blackjack table. I couldn't lose. From time to time, Tom would collect my chips and cash them in for me in small-enough batches not to attract the notice of the IRS, for which I felt no guilt in view of the government's failed attempt to steal the railroads in the Northeast from their owners and their successful attempt to steal five years of my life from me. I did well enough so that eventually one of the dragon ladies who functioned as a pit boss sidled over, inspecting me as closely as possible. "You seem to be having a really good night," she said.

"Look, lady, if you can't tell a lucky drunk from a card counter, you and I are both in the wrong business." She laughed. I wish I could have.

Epilogue

They're all dead now, mostly. The three judges of the Special Court; Joe Castle, after typically ignoring his doctor's order not to visit his daughter in Denver because of the altitude; Lock Fogg and Bill Hesse in the fullness of their years, fully vindicated as to the value of their railroad. Grant and Tom—Grant from too much alcohol over a long period of time, Tom from a surplus of cigarettes. Bill Dimeling and Jim Sox, way too young. Of the list of the fallen, two deaths affected me the most.

The first was Henry Friendly's. When I read of his suicide in March of 1986, I found myself sobbing uncontrollably, which was totally inexplicable since I never really knew him at all, not even to exchange as little as a civil greeting: "Good morning, Mr. Lewis." "Good morning, Your Honor." Our "relationship" consisted of my attempts to answer his unending stream of highly intelligent and provocative questions and make as clear and convincing as possible our arguments for the valuation of what I now felt to be my railroad, in view of my contribution to a legal proceeding he created, structured, and managed in order to solve one of the most complicated and novel legal problems ever to exist in American jurisprudence. In the course of the five years we were together (longer than many marriages), I became persuaded that he epitomized the best of my profession: extraordinary intelligence; a determination to work harder than anyone should; a willingness, indeed eagerness, to explore all the issues in the case; an ability to control the litigation so that it moved at an extraordinary pace without giving anyone cause to complain that they had not been heard; and of course, total honesty and integrity. The most vivid memory I have of him now is posthumous. Several years after Friendly's death and several years before his own, I entertained John Wisdom following a talk he gave at my request at the Historical Society of Pennsylvania, when he told me the following story in private: On the night he took the suicidal overdose of pills, Friendly wrote a number of letters. The one he wrote to Wisdom went something like this:

Dear John,

I have read your draft opinion in the matter of X [a case involving a Penn Central tariff dispute concerning grain shipments on the Great Lakes] and I agree with it entirely, but since it rests on a point not fully developed either in the briefs or at oral argument, I think it might be usefully reargued lest we give the impression of being arbitrary. I am sorry that I will not be able to assist you further in this matter.

Sincerely,

Henry J. Friendly.

By the way Judge Wisdom told me this story and the way he looked while telling it, I thought he was disappointed, that he expected either more or less, either some reflection on the nature of the law and their joint experience as two of the most highly regarded judges of their time thrown together for seven years of intense work, or nothing.

The second death that affected me more than any other was, of course, Jim's. After the Reading, it became clear to both of us that his real calling was not the law, but the Episcopalian ministry. What had been a strong interest became his life. I jokingly told him, "Mammon having failed you as far as compensation is concerned, you've decided to try God," and I also helped him with a little money toward completing his seminary training. I suppose one of the few really good things I got from the Reading case was his asking me to be one of the lay presenters at his ordination. I remember standing with his parents and his longtime lover (I hate the word "partner" for that relationship; as should be clear by now, "partner" to me has far different connotations than a deeply committed loving bond) when he did something totally corny: he took me in his arms and said, "Howard, you have only sons—this is your one chance to be father of the bride." When my older boy got engaged to be married and asked me who I thought should perform the ceremony, I strongly suggested Jim. He was delighted and my kids liked him, but tragically he got sick and had to drop out. He was dead in six months from kidney disease, despite his lover's attempt to save him by donating one of his kidneys.

There are some survivors besides myself. There is John Fowler, who worked with Bill Dimeling crafting the plan of reorganization. There is Judge William Ditter, who seems to be ageless, little changed since the reorganization. There is Drew Lewis, who after a brilliant job as Reagan's secretary of transportation very successfully turned Warner Amex around and revitalized the Union Pacific, a stunning series of untarnished successes. Thereafter, he seemed to fall apart, engaged in an unending struggle with alcohol, which to me is tragic, particularly in view of his truly brilliant former career and his obvious potential.

Despite myself and the few relics listed above, the Reading story is essentially one of decline and mortality. Except the trains. The trains are doing just fine. Before he became secretary of transportation, Drew told me and others that among his first priorities was to get the federal government out of the railroad business. In order to do that, two things had to happen: the claims by the bankrupt estates against the government had to be resolved and Conrail had to become profitable. Though, of course, as a former trustee of a bankrupt railroad he could not be directly involved in settling the cases, he let it be known to all of his staff at Transportation that this was what he wanted. In doing so, he reinforced the efforts of the Special Court, through its imposed accelerated trial schedule and not-so-subtle hints, to achieve the same ends. The second goal, Conrail profitability, was somewhat more elusive. It required that Conrail immediately get out of the commuter passenger responsibility and pass that albatross on to local authorities.[1] In Philadelphia, that meant the Southeastern Pennsylvania Transportation Authority (SEPTA), which was funded by the Commonwealth of Pennsylvania, the city of Philadelphia, and the four surrounding counties (Chester, Delaware, Bucks, and Montgomery), all of whom had previously provided inadequate support to the Reading and Penn Central and now had to assume total responsibility for the service. Second, the existing railroad labor contracts, which had been voided by the transfer of rail service from the bankrupts to Conrail, had to be renegotiated so that the former five-man crew of engineer, fireman, conductor, and two trainmen was reduced to two, an engineer and a conductor, and the antiquated work rules dating from the nineteenth century were eliminated. Also, all of a sudden the caboose disappeared. All of this happened in surprisingly short order without much labor opposition, since the unions relied on the labor protection provisions of the Rail Act.

In addition to these changes, the ICL had to be made more flexible in its ability to discontinue unprofitable roads and service with more expedition than the endless hearings and filings heretofore necessary. These were just the highlights of the transformation effected in a relatively short period.

Once Conrail had become profitable, the government engaged several large investment banks to effect an IPO to sell its stock to the public. The stock went out at $18.00 a share, and some dozen years later Conrail sold itself to the Chessie and the Norfolk Southern at $150.00 a share, which did not displease me personally as an early buyer of Conrail shares. Aside from my own profit I strongly believed, as someone forced to know more about railroads than he ever wanted to, that the combination was a great step forward for the economy in that it created two great systems in the East, Chessie and Norfolk Southern, which if they were then combined with the previously built two great systems in the West, Burlington Northern and Union Pacific, would make possible the two-system transcontinental rail service with its inherent efficiencies that Canada has enjoyed for almost a century.

As I survey the entire process from the commencement of the bankruptcy proceedings to the current state of rail transportation, the only word I can think of is triumph. It is a triumph of the bankruptcy system aided, but not dominated by, federal intervention. The government, the economy, all of us now have a rail transportation network that is infinitely better than it had been before the Penn Central bankruptcy, at a very moderate cost. The creditors got their compensation in accordance with their priorities, and in a few cases (notably the Reading) the stockholders found their faith in the basic value of the railroads vindicated. All of us came out of the process basically happy.

I began this memoir by asserting that the fate of the railroads in the Northeast embodied the best and worst of American law. The best was the happy resolution described above, stemming from the breakdown of the rail industry in the Northeast. The worst was the government's creation of the problem in the first instance. I firmly believe there would have been no railroad collapse absent the government's failure to realize what it was doing and that policies appropriate for dealing with particular problems must be adjusted as economic and demographic needs change over time. The Interstate Commerce Act and the commission it created were necessary in the nineteenth century to prevent railroad monopolies from demanding unreasonable tariffs to the detriment of the economy. The same policies and procedures were not appropriate for dealing with a totally different economy, including a great deal of government-subsidized competing modes of transportation. For the same reason, there was no need to succumb to the unreasonable demands of labor. In dealing with the railroads, the government demonstrated its persuasive tendency to rely on theoretical models (witness Obamacare) instead of looking at the rust on the cars.

Perhaps even more revealingly, the fate of the railroads from the mid-nineteenth century until the cataclysmic bankruptcies described herein illustrates the lack of flexibility of government when dealing with economic problems. It was necessary to create the ICL and prevent devastating labor strikes which might have caused severe national calamity, but once the institutions were created to deal with these problems, they acquired laws of their own and became insulated from reality.

There was one exception to the general euphoria surrounding the railroad outcome—railroad labor. The union reliance on the labor compensation provisions of the Rail Act proved misplaced, for what Congress gives, Congress can take away. The Omnibus Budget Reconciliation Act of 1981, passed after the government's settlement with the transferors and after the irrevocable takeover of rail operation by Conrail, limited the original open-ended obligation for compensation to twenty thousand dollars per person resulting from job elimination or twenty-five thousand for termination (Northeast Rail Service Act of 1981, Title VII, Sec. 701[d], Sec. 702[a]). The preamble to the act sums it up:

(4) the provisions for protection of employees of bankrupt railroads contained in the Regional Rail Reorganization Act of 1973 have resulted in the payment of benefits far in excess of those anticipated at the time of enactment, have imposed

an excessive fiscal burden on the Federal taxpayer, and are now an obstacle to the establishment of improved rail service and continued rail employment in the Northeast region of the United States; and

(5) since holding Conrail liable for employee protection payables would destroy its prospects of becoming a profitable carrier and further injure its employees, an alternative employee protection system must be developed and funded.

This passage is instructive on several levels. Not only does it point out the greatest flaw in the original Rail Act and detail its cause, but it also illustrates an often-employed subterfuge contained in legislation effecting fundamental change. The legislation is sold to Congress and the people as providing great improvement at very little cost. Then, when the real cost becomes evident some years later, Congress and the administration can avoid responsibility on the grounds that they weren't responsible for the legislation; they are only implementing it as required. Obamacare in concept is a quintessential example of this ploy carried to its ultimate extreme. Unfortunately for the proponents of the Rail Act, the problems have surfaced far earlier than anticipated, so that the authors have found mud on their faces far earlier than might have been expected.

In the interest of completeness, I suppose I should, in rather broad-brush terms, sketch what happened to me in the years following the valuation case. By and large, it is a rather typical happy story of gradual withdrawal and aging, though there were a few rough spots, particularly in the beginning. First, I began to get some control over my personal life. Shortly after the settlement's approval I was able to stop smoking. Unlike many, I found it relatively easy. The need for tobacco as a support had ended and no one else in my family smoked. I never quit smoking; I just said to myself, "Today I will not smoke." This has gone on now day by day for over thirty years. Alcohol has been another matter, but I have been able to cut back; there are fewer "bubble dourbons."

As far as my professional life is concerned, I found that the work I used to do for a variety of small to moderate-sized clients, which I entrusted to others in order to necessarily devote my full efforts to the Reading, had not been lent but given. New relationships had developed and it was not in my power, nor perhaps in the client's best interest, for me to attempt to reclaim them. As an aside, I believe that law firms that take major projects which are self-contained in nature with no follow-through do themselves a disservice if they do not make a conscious effort to redeploy the people who work on those projects after they come to an end; otherwise, the firm will not be able to find lawyers to take them on. I felt to some extent abandoned as well as dog-tired, without the energy to rebuild another practice.

This was the time, too, that I felt that in order to make up my loss of income due to diminished work, and despite the cushion provided by the Penn Central bond proceeds, I should consider asking for a premium fee based on the Reading success. I figured the guys from Chicago, unlike my partners, would welcome me with open arms, and that since I had made them $26 million, they might be glad to reward me with $1 million. I was wrong. It seems that the amount obtained wasn't really as high as it might have been; the case was a simple one that any first-year law student could have won; lawyers are just grasping parasites. Besides, despite their own personal inclination, they owed a fiduciary duty to the other shareholders. After some considerable back and forth, along with some much-appreciated urging from Joe and Drew, they came up with an offer of $350,000. Well, $350,000 is a lot better than nothing, and that is something one can't really fight about let alone litigate, so I thanked them profusely and accepted their generosity. After all, was I really any different (except in my own mind) from Pat Cestaro of Oppenheimer?

The next question after securing the $350,000 was how to divide the money between me and the firm. I felt that since I had worked most of my time on the Reading at ICC-mandated starvation rates, which was fully reflected in my diminished compensation, at least half the premium should be mine. Others felt differently. The management committee called a special partners' meeting to consider the matter, and I began to marshal my arguments on my behalf when Grant came into my office. "Howard," he said, "we think it would be unseemly for you to come in and make demands—it will only stir up bad feelings. Don't worry, Tom and I have enlisted Tony to plead your case." The upshot was that the partners, in their wisdom, decided to give me $25,000, or 7 percent. Without commenting on what happens when you give a waiter a 7 percent tip,

I accepted their heartfelt appreciation, gave half the money to Jim Sox to help cover his seminary expenses, and got drunk. No, I didn't spend quite all of the $12,500 on one glorious binge.

Shortly after receiving my dazzling bonus from my firm, I was sitting in my office trying to figure out what other cases I could dream up when once again Grant, this time joined by Tom, came into my office: "Howard, we have decided to leave this place and form a firm of our own, specializing in litigation and labor law, and we'd like you to join us as our sole corporate presence. When we saw how they [I found the use of this pronoun interesting under the circumstances] treated you in the Reading matter, we realized that there isn't any kindness or mutual support, let alone appreciation, here anymore." They asked me to go with them as a one-man Corporate Department of a firm to be called Sprecher, Felix, Visco, Hutchinson and Young, which didn't include a whole lot of people other than the named partners. I thought it over for about thirty seconds, realized that these guys were about the only friends I had at work and that I was done with the business of being part of managing a law firm, and said yes, provided I would be a contract employee and not a partner; I'd had enough of partnership. So for the next seven years I labored there cleaning up the Reading asbestos work, but more significantly I became involved in a difficult situation involving my best friend's insurance empire (empire?—well anyhow, freehold) and even more involved in the never-ending family trust and estate work. I am forever grateful to Jim Young for giving me, during that time, an opportunity rarely afforded a business lawyer: that of screwing both a bank (Bank of America) and a credit company (General Electric) on behalf of a fly-by-night packager of medical accessory loans (wheelchairs, hospital beds, and the like). But that was one of the few highs in an otherwise unrewarding practice.

I would have stayed at Sprecher, Felix longer, except that the firm collapsed. For years, beginning before we left Obermayer, Grant had fought an increasingly losing battle with alcohol, till one day he fell down dead drunk in open court. The judge looked down from the bench and said, "Gee, he was so good. I wonder what he would have been like sober." That, of course, was the end of his practice. The firm's collapse followed shortly on Grant's. His Litigation Department dispersed to various havens, large and small, while Tom moved his labor group en masse to

Montgomery McCracken Walker & Rhoads, where I later joined him. I remember, sometime before his final exit from the law, having a dry lunch with Grant in an effort to keep him sober and asking him, "Why are you doing this? Why are you destroying yourself?"

"Look, Howard, I leave a marriage which is virtually over in the morning to go to a job I can't stand all day, to return to the same lifeless marriage at night. The only thing that keeps me going is Scotch. I think I fell out of love with the law when people stopped saying thank you. The money, no matter what it is, isn't enough to compensate for the stress and commitment we put into this business. There has to be some psychic reward."

"I know what you mean about the thanks, but the process itself, the sense of providing the oil which allows this competitive entrepreneurial economy and diverse individualistic society to function, indeed thrive, has an appeal on its own, irrespective of whether you like or even care about the people you serve. I have a sense that without us, the whole structure might fall apart."

"Not for me. Not anymore."

Upon the dissolution of Sprecher, Felix, I thought that I might at last retire. The only real problem that remained was my insurance company client, since I found I could do the family work as a kind of sideline and had found others, including my lawyer son, to share it. In the insurance case, Grant had already won in binding arbitration the major fight brought by their client, the Mutual Assurance Company, which arguably my client had driven to bankruptcy. I had cleaned up the problems they had as managers of two other companies, and all that remained was a case brought by the accountants, Coopers and Lybrand, who accused us of misleading the Mutual Assurance Company, which was suing them. As he was staggering out the door, Grant handed me the file. There was absolutely nothing in it, and I was four years and ten thousand pages of depositions behind. I gulped, asked the client if they had room for me in their office, and became for a time a sole practitioner, doing little else but this lawsuit and the ever-present family work.

In a short time we settled with Coopers and together we and Coopers defeated the Mutual Assurance Company. Retirement now seemed to me to be in the offing, except that a good friend of mine who was having problems with his parents' estates asked me if I would join the law firm a great-uncle of his had co-founded, which was handling the matter. I was willing but I would await their invitation. In due course, it came, and I settled into practice at Montgomery McCracken Walker & Rhoads. Of all the places where I had worked, including working for myself, I found Montgomery to be by far the most collegial and civilized. The firm demonstrates that you don't have to be a shit, surrounded by shits, to practice law effectively, occasionally brilliantly.

The Reading also eased itself into retirement as an important constituent of Conrail, but its function as an operating entity ceased. With its passing into Conrail, I no longer hated trains but have come to view the whole industry with a kind of nostalgia. As I survey my now fifty years of practice from a vantage point where I can work at my own pace and do what I now do best—attract clients for other, more able lawyers to service—I remember an old Irish blessing: "May your road be always downhill and the wind always at your back."

NOTES

FOREWORD

1. The word "Railroad" does not appear in the Reading Company's formal name. However, the company often explicated its functional purpose by including the words "Reading Railway System" as either a prefix or a subtitle in passenger service timetables and other company publications and advertisements.

INTRODUCTION

1. The history of the Reading is well described in James L. Holton, *The Reading Railroad: History of a Coal Age Empire*, 2 vols. (Lewisburg, PA: Garrigues House, 1989–1992).

4. THE BEGINNING

1. The reference is to Daniel Webster's opening to his nine-hour argument before the Supreme Court in the Dartmouth College case: "I represent Dartmouth College. It is but a small college, but there are those of us who love it."

5. THE PLOT THICKENS

1. *In the Matter of the Valuation Proceedings under §§303(c) and 306 of the Regional Rail Reorganization Act*, 439 F. Supp. 1351 (1977).

2. *In the Matter of the Valuation Proceedings under §§303(c) and 306 of the Regional Rail Reorganization Act*, 445 F. Supp. 994 (1977).

3. David M. Dorsen, *Henry Friendly, Greatest Judge of His Era* (Cambridge, MA: Belknap Press of Harvard University Press, 2012), 293.

6. FEAR AND EXHAUSTION

1. Dorsen, *Henry Friendly, Greatest Judge of His Era.*

11. END GAME

1. I feel obliged to digress at this point, because the case against legal obfuscation is something of a crusade with me. At one point in my life I was lead outside bond counsel to the city of Philadelphia, not because of any talent of mine but because my then-partner Marty Weinberg was Mayor Frank Rizzo's best friend. Typically, when the city borrowed money by way of a bond issue sold through underwriters to the public, it pledged pieces of city real estate or an income stream derived from the property. The city/issuer was enjoined from abandoning, selling, hocking, pledging to other lenders, or failing to maintain the property. The in-

denture embodying this great and subtle concept usually read as follows: "With respect to the Collateral, the issuer shall not abandon, abort, abridge, arbitrate . . . bargain away, besmirch, besmuck, bemoan . . . condemn, convey, conflate, commingle, confuse, cohabit . . . defame, debauch, debunk, destroy, deter . . . escheat, encumber, enface, eliminate, encapsulate . . . forfeit, forswear, foreclose, forestall . . . harm, hurt, hinder, harass, harvest . . . sell, sacrifice, surrender, subpoena, surprise . . . or otherwise alienate any indicia of ownership." That lovely piece of prose is always met with the question, "What precisely do you mean by indicia?" and there goes supper, let alone drinks. If anyone thinks that is a silly hyperbolic caricature, I encourage him or her to read, or try to read, the Affordable Care Act.

EPILOGUE

1. The intercity long-distance passenger rail service had long before been transferred to the federal government in the creation of Amtrak.

BOOKS IN THE RAILROADS PAST AND PRESENT SERIES

Landmarks on the Iron Road: Two Centuries of North American Railroad Engineering by William D. Middleton

South Shore: The Last Interurban (revised second edition) by William D. Middleton

Katy Northwest: The Story of a Branch Line Railroad by Don L. Hofsommer

"Yet there isn't a train I wouldn't take": Railway Journeys by William D. Middleton by William D. Middleton

The Pennsylvania Railroad in Indiana by William J. Watt

In the Traces: Railroad Paintings of Ted Rose by Ted Rose

A Sampling of Penn Central: Southern Region on Display by Jerry Taylor

The Lake Shore Electric Railway Story by Herbert H. Harwood Jr. and Robert S. Korach

The Pennsylvania Railroad at Bay: William Riley McKeen and the Terre Haute & Indianapolis Railroad by Richard T. Wallis

The Bridge at Québec by William D. Middleton

History of the J. G. Brill Company by Debra Brill

Uncle Sam's Locomotives: The USRA and the Nation's Railroads by Eugene L. Huddleston

Metropolitan Railways: Rapid Transit in America by William D. Middleton

Perfecting the American Steam Locomotive by J. Parker Lamb

From Small Town to Downtown: A History of the Jewett Car Company, 1893–1919 by Lawrence A. Brough and James H. Graebner

Limiteds, Locals, and Expresses in Indiana, 1838–1971 by Craig Sanders

Steel Trails of Hawkeyeland: Iowa's Railroad Experience by Don L. Hofsommer

Amtrak in the Heartland by Craig Sanders

When the Steam Railroads Electrified (revised second edition) by William D. Middleton

The GrandLuxe Express: Traveling in High Style by Karl Zimmermann

Still Standing: A Century of Urban Train Station Design by Christopher Brown

The Indiana Rail Road Company: America's New Regional Railroad by Christopher Rund

Evolution of the American Diesel Locomotive by J. Parker Lamb

The Men Who Loved Trains: The Story of Men Who Battled Greed to Save an Ailing Industry by Rush Loving Jr.

The Train of Tomorrow by Ric Morgan

Built to Move Millions: Streetcar Building in Ohio by Craig R. Semsel

The CSX Clinchfield Route in the 21st Century by Jerry Taylor and Ray Poteat

The New York, Westchester & Boston Railway: J. P. Morgan's Magnificent Mistake by Herbert H. Harwood Jr.

Iron Rails in the Garden State: Tales of New Jersey Railroading by Anthony J. Bianculli

Visionary Railroader: Jervis Langdon Jr. and the Transportation Revolution by H. Roger Grant

The Duluth South Shore & Atlantic Railway: A History of the Lake Superior District's Pioneer Iron Ore Hauler by John Gaertner

Iowa's Railroads: An Album by H. Roger Grant and Don L. Hofsommer

Frank Julian Sprague: Electrical Inventor and Engineer by William D. Middleton and William D. Middleton III

Twilight of the Great Trains (expanded edition) by Fred W. Frailey

Little Trains to Faraway Places by Karl Zimmermann

Railroad Noir: The American West at the End of the Twentieth Century by Linda Grant Niemann

From Telegrapher to Titan: The Life of William C. Van Horne by Valerie Knowles

The Railroad That Never Was: Vanderbilt, Morgan, and the South Pennsylvania Railroad by Herbert H. Harwood Jr.

Boomer: Railroad Memoirs by Linda Grant Niemann

Indiana Railroad Lines by Graydon M. Meints

The Indiana Rail Road Company: America's New Regional Railroad (revised and expanded edition) by Christopher Rund, Fred W. Frailey, and Eric Powell

The CSX Clinchfield Route in the 21st Century (now in paperback) by Jerry Taylor and Ray Poteat

Wet Britches and Muddy Boots: A History of Travel in Victorian America by John H. White Jr.

Landmarks on the Iron Road: Two Centuries of North American Railroad Engineering (now in paperback) by William D. Middleton

On Railways Far Away by William D. Middleton

Railroads of Meridian by J. Parker Lamb, with contributions by David H. Bridges and David S. Price

Railroads and the American People by H. Roger Grant

The Electric Pullman: A History of the Niles Car and Manufacturing Company by Lawrence A. Brough

John Frank Stevens: Civil Engineer by Clifford Foust

Off the Main Lines: A Photographic Odyssey by Don L. Hofsommer

The Rock Island Line by Bill Marvel

The Railroad That Never Was: Vanderbilt, Morgan, and the South Pennsylvania Railroad (now in paperback) by Herbert H. Harwood, Jr.

The Louisville, Cincinnati & Charleston Rail Road: Dreams of Linking North and South by H. Roger Grant

The Iowa Route: A History of the Burlington, Cedar Rapids & Northern Railway by Don L. Hofsommer

The Lake Shore Electric Railway Story (now in paperback) by Herbert H. Harwood Jr. and Robert S. Korach

Railroaders without Borders: A History of the Railroad Development Corporation by H. Roger Grant

A graduate of Harvard Law School, HOWARD H. LEWIS continues to practice law after over fifty years. He lives outside Philadelphia, Pennsylvania.

JOHN C. SPYCHALSKI is Professor Emeritus of Supply Chain Management at the Pennsylvania State University. Railroad industry–related issues and conditions have long been of prime focus in his professional work.